futureTHINK Press | Alberta Teachers' Association

Rethinking School Leadership - Creating Great Schools for *All* Students

J-C Couture, PhD and Stephen Murgatroyd, PhD, FBPsS, FRSA

© futureTHINK Press, 2012

© 2012 future**THINK** Press. All rights reserved

The phrase **Rethinking The Future**™ is trademarked to the Innovation Expedition Inc. and may not be used without permission.

The rights of J-C Couture and Stephen Murgatroyd to be identified as the editors of this work have been asserted according to the U.S. Copyright, Designs and Patent Act of 1988 and appropriate Canadian copyright law.

The rights of Philip McRae, J-C Couture, Pasi Sahlberg, Stephen Murgatroyd, C. Naylor, Jim Parsons, Christine Stobart, Bobbi Compton, Melissa Humby, Raime Drake, Karen Lam, Dennis Shirley, Jean Stiles, and Shirley Stiles to be identified as authors of materials in this collection this work have been asserted according to the U.S. Copyright, Designs and Patent Act of 1988 and appropriate Canadian copyright law.

Printed in the United States of America.

No part of this publication may be reproduced, stored in or introduced into a retrieval system, or transmitted in any form, or by means (electronic, mechanical, photocopying, recording, or otherwise) without prior written permission of the publisher. Requests for permission should be addressed to future**THINK** Press, the Innovation Expedition Inc., 7608 150 Street, Edmonton, Alberta T5R 1C8, Canada.

Couture, J-C 1955-
Murgatroyd, Stephen 1950-

Rethinking School Leadership - Creating Great Schools for All Students

ISBN: 978-1-105-68536-1

If you are interested in these ideas, please visit www.learningourway.ca

Table of Contents

About the Authors 2

Preface 6

Teacher Leadership as an Intended Consequence of School Improvement: Sustaining an Ethic of "Gentle Action" 16

The Finnish Case 28

Teacher Leadership in Navigating the Multiple Spaces that Support Inclusion 50

Teacher Leadership in Action: Prospects and Perils? 72

Inside-Out Leadership in Two Schools: Owning our practice as leaders in learning 96

Fourth Way FINAL: The Power of the Internationalization of Networks of School Leaders 112

Conclusion 138

(Re)Thinking Leadership in a Digital Age: Perspectives, Provocations and Actions 142

Conclusion 162

The School as a Centre for Perpetual Innovation 170

Conclusion 197

Appendix One 200

Purpose of the Dialogue 201

The Key Challenge: What Makes for a Great School? 202

Background 202

Eight Key Challenges 209

About the Authors

Bobbi Compton is a primary school teacher in Fort McMurray, Alberta who is currently a learning coach for ATA, Local 48., Dr. K. A. Clark Public School in Fort McMurray Alberta. She is presently completing her Masters of Education in the Masters of Educational Studies Program (MES) at the University of Alberta.

J-C Couture is Associate Coordinator, Research with the Alberta Teachers' Association. His most recent publications focus on teachers' work life and school improvement. He is actively engaged in the Association's strategic planning work and collaboration with international partners on educational development projects.

Raime Drake is a teacher at Eleanor Hall School, Clyde, Alberta.

Melissa Humby is a teacher at Buck Mountain Central School, Buck Lake, Alberta.

Karen Lam following her successful completion of the Masters in Curriculum Studies at the Institute of Education, University of London, Karen worked in the development of the secondary and high school geography curriculum at the Ministry of Education, Singapore. She then joined the Curriculum Policy and Pedagogy Unit, which was set up in 2006 to catalyze and support school-based curriculum innovation among schools in Singapore. She is currently completing her doctoral studies at the Lynch School of Education, Boston College.

Phil McRae is an Executive Staff Officer with the Alberta Teachers' Association and Adjunct Professor within the Faculty of Education at the University of Alberta where he earned his Ph.D. He was the Director of the Alberta Initiative for School Improvement (AISI) at the University of Alberta from 2005-2009. Phil has worked in many secondary and post-secondary educational contexts while living and teaching in the Middle East (United Arab Emirates), Asia (Japan), Europe (Spain), and in Alberta, Canada with the Lethbridge Public School District and on the Blood (Kainai) Reservation.

Stephen Murgatroyd is a management consultant, writer and publisher. His most recent books include Renaissance Leadership - Rethinking and Leading the Future (2010) Rethinking Education – Learning and the New Renaissance (2011) and Rethinking the Future – Six Patterns Shaping the New Renaissance (2012). He has worked extensively on school based leadership and innovation projects since the early 1970's.

Charles Naylor is a research officer with the British Columbia Teachers' Federation.

Jim Parsons is Professor of Education at the University of Alberta, Faculty of Education.

Pasi Sahlberg is Director General of the Centre for International Mobility and Cooperation at the Finnish Ministry of Education and Culture. He is the author of *Finnish Lessons – What Can the World Learn from Educational Change in Finland?* (Teachers College Press, 2011).

Dennis Shirley is Professor at the Lynch School of Education at Boston College. His work ranges from assisting beginning teachers in complex school environments to designing large scale research and intervention projects for school districts and States.

He is evaluating the partnership between Finland and Alberta focused on the next stage in the development of their school systems.

P. Jean Stiles was a teacher, consultant and has been principal of four Edmonton Public Schools. She is now Principal of Jasper Place High School.

Shirley Stiles was a teacher, principal and senior staff school administrator with the Edmonton Public School Board. She is now an international consultant on improving student learning.

Christine Stobart is both a University Facilitator with the Faculty of Education, Field Experiences, and a Teaching Assistant within the Master of Educational Studies program at the University of Alberta. She is currently pursuing her Ed.D. at the University of Calgary.

Preface

We began, prompted by the late Chris Gonnet, Superintendent of Grande Prairie Public Schools, to explore the question *What Makes a Great School?* in December 2010 at a meeting in Boston. We concluded that it involved many inter-connected elements, but that the key components were focused teacher leadership enabled by being empowered and resourced to make a difference. *Rethinking Leadership* sees evidence-informed practice as the fulcrum point for leveraging school improvement, especially if it systematically supported within a systematic way at the jurisdiction and provincial levels to build school leadership capacity.

We also concluded that the framing conditions for the work of the school – the provincial/state policies, curriculum requirements, financial arrangements, assessment regimes as well as the policies of school boards and districts – either enables or impairs the ability of a team within the school to create a great school for all students.

These basic (and seemingly simple) insights led to a major conference in Edmonton, Alberta, March 2011, involving some three hundred educators, policy makers (including a cabinet Minister from the Alberta Government) and others to meet to discuss the question, using a challenge dialogue that several of the authors of the materials in this book, as well as Chris Gonnet, contributed to (we provide this 2011 document in Appendix One). Also present at this meeting were colleagues from Finland

– the start of our partnership between Alberta teachers, students and policy makers with their counterparts from Finland, a partnership that remains vibrant, persistent and providing opportunities for school based innovation.

The idea that a great school can be had for *all* is at first brush, seemingly a simplistic catch-phrase. Yet at its core we see it is as a hopeful provocation. It is a challenge that invites educational leaders to address these questions:

1. How do we ensure equity for all learners – no matter what their home conditions, physical or mental challenges or levels of support in the community?
2. How do we provide learning pathways which meet the different needs of different learners while at the same time ensuring the quality of all learning taking place in the school?
3. How do we leverage the assets of a community to enable all to learn in a school?
4. How do we leverage technology to support engaged and inclusive learning for all?
5. How do we enable schools to design learning pathways for each student so that their ambitions, hopes and opportunities are realized?

These are not easy questions and we do not answer them in this collection of materials. We do, however, explore them as hopeful provocations that call upon school leaders to become their best selves. Such a moral imperative honours the sacred trust we are called to every day so aptly described by Wayne Hulley: "Parents send the best kids that they have to our schools."

We explore these questions from a simple starting point. Educational change and development – real change – takes place in a school, in a classroom and with students and teachers engaged in real learning. This is where we should look to reform, change and development: it is where "the rubber hits the road", where the genuine and mindful action is. *Rethinking Leadership* shares the few that a simplistic, one-size-fits-all approach to system leadership ultimately does not control *what people do*, but what people *cannot do* (Kanter, 1977). If we want to support innovation in schools, such an approach rewards cultures of sufficiency ('it is good enough') rather than culture of shared risk-tasking and transformation ('we can become better selves').

This collection of ~~short~~ chapters explores the question: What does teacher leadership look like in schools which seek to be great for *all* students? The chapters are varied both in tone and texture – representing a rich complexity of school-communities. Some chapters are written by those who advise, research and support schools. Others are written or co-written by those who work in schools. Each contribution seeks to better understand the challenge of being a teacher leader or a leader or teachers in a school. Each chapter engages the complex task of describing the ephemeral qualities ascribed to leadership in schools in the context of the uncertainty and volatility that increasingly characterizes life in schools today.

In the opening paper, J-C Couture and Pasi Sahlberg explore the idea of "gentle action" – an idea on loan from David Peat's 2008 book *Gentle Action – Bringing Creative Change to a Turbulent World*. They conclude that teacher leadership will continue to be what it has always been: creating possibility where there seems to be only limitation. With examples from both Alberta and Finland, they illustrate this idea in action. Seeing teacher leadership as a "soulcraft", they offer insights as to how and why this must be developed and supported in a systemic way.

C. (Charlie) Naylor from the B.C. Teachers' Federation explores the idea of teacher leadership with respect to social inclusion. With practical examples of what supports have been made available to teachers in British Columbia, he provides insights of what teachers can do when empowered, supported and enabled.

Jim Parsons, Christine Stobart, Bobbi Compton, Melissa Humby and Raime Drake describe in some detail what happens when innovation is attempted by committed and focused teacher leaders in schools. Five specific change projects and their aftermath are described and not all went well, as you will see. They offer cautionary tales from experience, yet point to real gains in terms of the intent to make schools a great place for all students.

Jean Stiles and Shirley Stiles, the current and a former principal of Alberta's largest high school, compare and contrast their experience of supporting the development of teacher leaders in two very different contexts. One example is a rural school in northern Alberta that represents so many school-communities trying to meet the challenge of offering rich project-based learning for students in a small school. The second example represents significant contrast: the largest high school in Alberta that is exploring ways to differentiate learning opportunities for all students that honours different ways of knowing and being in the world.

Karen Lam and Dennis Shirley from the Lynch School of Education at Boston College, who are engaged in the evaluation of the Finland-Alberta Partnership, explore what this partnership is leading to now and what it could mean for the future of both school systems. Observing that change always looks better at the macro level of a government agency than it does at the micro level of the school, they look at tangible outcomes at the school and district level of the partnership and the challenge of making change stick. They suggest specific actions which could further support effective change at the level of the school.

Phil McRae explores the implications of digital technologies for leadership and change within the school. His focus is on student engagement through inquiry based learning, building communities of learners (students, teachers, administrators) and avoiding the pitfalls of an obsession with technology.

Stephen Murgatroyd, who has been active in teacher led change since the 1970's in South Wales, England and Alberta, provides a framework for thinking about the work of innovation and change. He links this to a case study and shows the steps involved in making change happen and the demanding work of making change sustainable. He also describes some of the necessary conditions for sustained teacher leadership.

We provide an Appendix with some tools to help those in school to use as resources for effective teacher leadership and point to other tools that may be of value.

This book is meant to stimulate a conversation about what makes a great school for all students and what teacher leaders can do to create and support such a school. It does not answer all of the questions; we simply want to provide resources to support a "better" and more focused conversation given the unprecedented challenges and opportunities we face here in Alberta. Given the growing complexity of school-communities and diversity of students in our schools, a strategic focus on developing teacher leadership must become a priority. And while administrator and leadership development will remain important, research and committed action on producing teacher leaders must gain prominence in the decade ahead. The moral imperative is evident to many: the hierarchical and bureaucratic cultures that typify too many school systems today must be replaced by a realization that teacher leadership will ensure that schools become places of creativity and ingenuity.

A far more stark reality is also calling us to act. Based on the conservative estimate that 10,000 new teachers entered the profession in the past four years in this province (out of a total teaching force of 30,000). As these teachers gain experience and advance in their career trajectories, there can be no excuse for not making access to leadership development (including graduate programs, training institutes) a singular priority. Over two decades ago, in his now classic analysis of why reform efforts too often fall short, Seymour Sarason observed that "it is virtually impossible to create and sustain over time conditions for productive learning for students when they do not exist for teachers" (1990, p. 145). We must capitalize on the demographic transformation underway in Alberta schools by developing the leadership capacity of our changing teaching force by creating schools where leadership development is supported and sustained as a strategic priority.

We anticipate that these chapters will remind us that rethinking leadership in schools must be immunized against sloganeering and becoming appropriated by so many "leadership adjectives" that slip and slide in the literature (Leithwood, 2004(a); 2004(b) such as *distributed leadership, instructional leadership,* and *transformational leadership*. More recently we see this slippage in some policy circles with talk of "technology leadership" as a discrete set of attributes. Rather than such a reductionist view of leadership, these chapters evoke the truism that effective leadership in healthy organizations is always a highly relational human activity: by definition it is about an individual having an influence *on* and *with* other human beings.

The literature on effective organizational improvement strategies underscores time and again that shared leadership "is about learning as a community" (Stoll, Fink and Earl, 2003, p. 132). Collaborative practitioner research in a learning community is more than a clever turn-of-phrase: in order for schools to learn, community must come first. We must remind ourselves that we must think of "learning" and "community" in multiple possibilities if we are to succeed in our goal: "learning of community; learning from community; learning with community; learning for community; and learning as community" (p. 134). In vibrant schools that are hubs of their communities, school leaders invariably realize that local problems are inextricably connected to larger societal challenges and global forces (Herr and Anderson, 2005, p. 67).

As we write this, governments around the world are looking at systems change and educational reform and transformation. We wish them every success. Our reality here is simple. Such changes mean nothing if they do not inspire teachers and teacher leaders to act. The experiences documented here of great things happening in schools – every chapter has examples – show what teacher leaders can do under all sorts of conditions. They also speak to what gets in the way of allowing a school to be great for all students.

References

Herr, K. and G. Anderson. 2005. The Action Research Dissertation. London: Sage.

Kanter, R.M. 1977. Men and Women of the Corporation. New York: Basic Books.

Leithwood, P.; McAdie, N. Bascia, and A. Rodique 2004 (a). Teaching for deep understanding: towards the Ontario curriculum we need. Elementary Teachers' Federation of Ontario.

Leithwood, Kenneth, et al. (2004) (b). How leadership influences student learning: Learning from Leadership Project. University of Minnesota and University of Toronto.

Sarason, Seymour, B. 1990. The Predictable Failure of Education Reform. San Francisco: Jossey-Bass. p. 145

Stoll, L. D Fink and L. Earl. 2003. It's About Learning (and It's About Time). London: RoutledgeFalmer.

Teacher Leadership as an Intended Consequence of School Improvement: Sustaining an Ethic of "Gentle Action"

J-C Couture and Pasi Sahlberg

> *We are looking for a teacher who is safe and clear in leadership, who wants to work together with teams, works thematically and across subjects, lets students have influence over education and believes in the creative process as a tool for learning.*
>
> *(Advertisement in a Swedish newspaper as quoted in Sahlberg & Oldroyd, 2010)*

Introduction

Teacher leadership has become a new wall on which to lean the ladder of school reform efforts. While initially, the advertisement above might seem a bit odd or colloquial to a North American audience, perhaps it provides an important signal to which we ought to pay close attention.

In what follows, we examine how 'teacher leadership' is very much an emergent phenomenon, although this now almost current catch-phrase has not yet fully found coherent meaning in either the lived worlds of teachers, or the policy musings of school and system leaders in Alberta (if not internationally). Through two stories of teachers from Alberta and Finland who have emerged as leaders in their schools, we will outline some key elements that might help shape teacher leadership as a focused policy priority within the context of emerging research on distributed leadership (Mascall & Leithwood, 2008; Harris, 2009). While the literature provides considerable insights about the interpersonal skills and attributes of teacher leaders - such as their commitment to inquiry and organizational skills - there is a need to further understand the fluidity and volatility characteristic of the emerging and elusive trope of 'the teacher leader.'

Patterns of teacher leadership have been clearly articulated (Mascall, Leithwood, Straus & Sacks, 2008, 215-216) that underscore the need to develop a more systematic approach to nurturing and sustaining teacher leaders: ranging from "planful alignment, spontaneous alignment, spontaneous misalignment and anarchistic misalignment". The complex variables contributing to this spectrum of school and system approaches to distributed leadership deserve further attention. Two exemplars of emergent teacher leaders (drawn from Alberta and Finland) will be viewed through the conceptual frames offered by two social philosophers: Albert Borgmann (1992) and David Peat (2008).

The Alberta Case
According to an international consensus panel that reviewed the Alberta Initiative for School Improvement (AISI), this innovative approach to school development has demonstrated the power of distributed leadership, representing a profound cultural shift in the province's schools.

Along with changes in teaching have come shifts in how leadership is developed in schools. Leadership has come to include and encourage greater teacher leadership (Lieberman & Miller, 2004; Katzenmeyer & Moller, 2001) and distributed leadership (Harris, 2008; Spillane, 2006) – not everywhere and not always – but by taking on roles as consultants and coordinators and by securing slots of time in school to coach and mentor colleagues, teachers have increasingly spread their wings to be leaders of other teachers. Leadership is no longer confined to the principal's or superintendent's office but is increasingly being spread throughout the professional community, where it retains a close connection to classroom learning. (Hargreaves, Crocker, Davis, McEwen, Sahlberg, Sumara, Shirley, & Hughes (2009) p.100)

Hargreaves et al. illustrate the complex interplay between school, district and provincial variables that contribute to (or sometimes diminish) capacity building for formal and informal teacher leadership:

> *Formal Leadership*: Some AISI projects rely heavily on teachers promoted into coordinator roles and this raises the question but also the opportunity of developing internal leadership capacity behind them in their schools when they move into the district office.
>
> *Informal leadership*: Other districts develop more creative uses of teacher leadership by buying proportions of time of multiple teachers so they can also experience leadership

> with and of their colleagues without abandoning their classroom roles and leadership of students (p.100).

In both scenarios, the success in AISI projects seems to depend strongly on the effectiveness of principal- and superintendent-level leadership within the district. However, as Hargreaves et al. found, some districts benefited from outstanding leadership of more than one kind. Those jurisdictions that appeared to struggle or falter "had high-level leadership that was weak, excessively controlling and inflexible, or isolated from other schools and districts" (p. 100). In the study's view, "[T]he impact of AISI projects depended strongly on prior leadership capacity in being able to create a sense of direction and purpose and unleash the innovation and connectivity among professionals across the system" (p. 100).

Hargreaves et al. go on to stress the imperative for district leaders to support teacher leadership through a moral commitment "to shared leadership or distributed leadership" which "does not only call for more teacher leadership, but also requires sophisticated levels of inner strength, courage and confidence among high level leaders" (p. 100).

In closing their report, the authors put forward key recommendations that this chapter will pursue:

- *Make leadership development a clear AISI project priority* and desired outcome, not an assumed precondition of success. This means sharpening the leadership emphasis even further in the fourth cycle of funding for AISI.

- *Continue to affirm and expand the role and density of teacher leadership* in AISI schools, balancing the needs of district coordination with the continuation of leadership capacity building within schools.
- *Provide specific training and support for principals and district level leaders*, in conjunction with their professional associations, in relation to network leadership and the development of shared responsibility for change.
- *Promote focused interaction and networking among and across school leaders and district leaders,* that are characterized by mutual support, candid discussion, honest recognition of differences in degrees of success and implementation, clear protocols that promote critical dialogue, and open professional interaction in a culture of collaboration, inquiry and commitment to improvement (pp. 120-121).

Alberta is unique among Canadian provinces in many ways, including the structure of its education system; characterized by the highly collegial relationship that exists among members of the school community as they work together to create positive learning experiences for students. A crucial aspect of this relationship is the professional collaboration that exists between teachers and administrators. The introduction of the AISI has been an important complement to this collegial culture and focus on distributed leadership. It is against this provincial backdrop that we point to the experience of a young teacher, Kelly, in what follows.[1]

Teacher leadership as Soulcraft

Kelly, a fourth grade teacher who teaches at a large rural elementary school in the community of central Alberta, has three years of teaching experience and is excited about her new role as the grade four team-leader. To Kelly's six female colleagues, three of whom teach part-time, her work is especially important "because I have the most experience of anyone in the group". The team's two goals for the year are to:

i) focus on consistency in grade-level expectations in language arts and;
ii) share in the development of performance tasks that will help build consistent assessment practices.

A key scaffold for team's work is the triangulation of evidence of student learning (based on the work of Anne Davies[2]) derived from:

i) observation (of student behaviours and learning);
ii) products (student's assignments, tests); and
iii) conversations (with students and about their reflections of their work).

---

[1] Kelly is a pseudonym, as is the location of the school.
[2] Adapted from Anne Davies is drawn
http://www.annedavies.com/assessment_for_learning_ar_bap.html

Meeting each Thursday morning for 80 minutes, the team feels that the embedded professional development time "has been a life-saver since we didn't get a chance to question what we thought grade three writing looked like until we really began to look at all the ways grade three writing can be grade three writing – if that makes sense".

For Kelly and her team, the ongoing "puzzling through all the angles through which you talked about the students" was a focal point for their ongoing conversations. "Many times I felt I was in this really great predicament – I wanted to know the answer to questions about the quality of a student's work, but realized more and more that our team was about talking through this stuff".

Observation of student behavior/activity

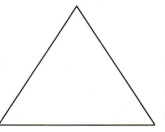

Conversations with students focussed on reflections about their work.

Products for peer examination of students' work

How does Kelly see her leadership role in the "puzzling through" of the questions related to student assessment? How did Kelly find herself in what she calls "this great predicament I am in"? "My job at our meetings is to help the group filter out the noise of the day-to-day things that easily distract us from the work".

She also sees her work as a sort of complement to her principal's (Louise), role as an "incredible administrator who makes our work as teachers possible". Kelly describes Louise as a principal who "just finds ways to make us better at what we do; if we need more planning time or a resource person to come and help us with a diagnostic assessment, then Louise finds a way to make it happen."

Looking back on the day Louise asked her to take on the team-leader role, Kelly admits "I was confused since I did not have the experience for this kind of thing – I mean running a meeting and developing a team work plan for the year". In fact, as Kelly recounts, "when Louise first set-up the 'AISI team', I still remember not paying close attention in the first meeting where it was introduced and sitting through two meetings before I had the courage to ask what 'AISI' meant. A colleague thought it might stand for the 'Assessment Indicators of Student something or other.'"

Kelly continually reinforces the sentiment that "no issues are too big or too small for us to pull together on – from the heavy questions about what a grade level means to how to futz with our district's electronic grade book that is full of technical bugs".

A compelling part of the grade-team's work is the book study they undertook of Matthew Crawford's (2009) *Shop Class as Soulcraft – An Inquiry into the Value of Work*. A philosopher and motorcycle shop owner, Crawford calls upon the education community to rekindle the 'craftsmanship' approach to human agency: where knowledge and competence are connected to daily work with one's hands, and engagement with the immediacy of the world. He calls into question the educational reforms and contrived standards that have created artificial environments for students, disengaging them from the (sometimes) intractable problems of the world. To truly take up one's soulcraft is to "dwell in the unease" (p. 9) of day-to-day challenges that require patient vigour and moral commitment to do the job right.

Kelly introduced the book to the group because it reminded her "so much of why I like repairing motorcycles – it just keeps me focussed on something I love - futzing". One of Kelly's favourite passages in Crawford's work is the invocation to acknowledge "the debt we owe to the world" and "to live wakefully is to live in full awareness of this, our human situation" (p. 208). Reluctant initially to bring the book into the group, Kelly recounts how "now everybody sees the point of a lot of work as teachers – just being there and staying focussed". As she looks around at her colleagues and students, she wonders, "We just can't walk away from the tough questions in our school – or like we are all tempted to do now: hit the 'DELETE' button on stuff we can't control".

There can be little doubt that in Kelly's case, the space and time afforded her by the AISI funding has been a vital part of her professional growth as a team leader. While there are many complex reasons contributing to her sense of leadership as a sort of 'soulcraft', part of her journey resonates in the work of the social philosopher Robert Borgmann, who coined the term "focal practice" (1992).

For Borgmann, the practice of professional work in an increasingly complex world calls for a combination of a deep emotional engagement in the innumerable and invisible things that a skilled professional skillfully does; driven by the moral imperative to make a positive difference in the life of someone else. But as Kelly reflects on those early days, "I went from thinking I had to rely on myself totally for knowing everything to realizing that we brought each other along…even sometimes when we weren't sure that was good enough – we always kept checking with each other". This was especially true for the 'part-timers' and the two teachers who came back from maternity leave. " I suddenly realized into my third year when I was the most senior member of the grade four team that there was no one else coming – I was the only one".

Borgmann evocatively reminds us that the word "focus" derives from the Latin, "hearth" – a gathering place that brings individuals together in a convivial way. He describes these places in ways that are everyday taken-for-granted examples but powerful reminders of the importance of being drawn together for a common cause – such as a local hockey rink in the midst of a cold Alberta winter. In cases of focal realism, the "rich reality…sponsors a sense of community" and become places where "reality and community conspire…" (p. 135).

For professional learning communities in Alberta schools, the evocative image of 'conspiring communities' points to understanding the difference between mere educational buzzwords and slogans such as "continuous improvement" and "accountability", and a more authentic appreciation for the power and warmth of focally real things in our schools such as professional responsibility as a form of soulcraft.

For example, Borgmann points to the difference between a modern central heating plant that mechanically warms a building and the power of a fireplace or hearth (p. 42). In the former case, a central heating plant is a machine or device that removes community from the necessity of coming together to keep warm. By contrast, in the case of the hearth, the fireplace compels individuals to socially gather. By removing individuals from the immediate need to build and tend to the fire together, central heating diminishes community and conviviality. For Borgmann, it is the conversations around the fire where we find community and the emergence of meaning – not the fire itself. "A (focal) practice keeps faith with focal things and saves them for an opening in our lives" (p. 209). It is in bringing teachers together to inquire about ways to improve student learning that AISI represents a focal practice.

As we have seen in the literature, "teacher leadership" can easily lapse into empty sloganeering where catch-phrases substitute for real meaning and significance in the lives of students and teachers (Hargreaves and Fink, 2006). For these writers, authentic professional inquiry thrives only if it is supported by a comprehensive set of supports at the school level, such as depth and conservation strategies. Depth strategies consider the need for deep and real learning in schools by recognizing that inventiveness and ingenuity are fostered through attention to conservation; through slow learning, focused on locally determined priorities and needs. In this sense, professional learning is connected to the emotional engagement as well as the intellectual growth of teachers.

The literature on organizational improvement underscores time and again that "it is about learning as a community" (Stoll, Fink and Earl 2003, p.132). In Kelly's case, teacher leadership in facilitating collaborative-practitioner research in a learning community is more than a clever turn of phrase. In order for schools to learn, relationships in a community must come first. In Kelly's case, the moral courage and personal sense of efficacy needed to push forward with her colleagues was equally impressive as it was unacknowledged by the school staff. We must reflect on the many leadership roles teachers enact so as to succeed in our goal of "learning of community; learning from community; learning with community; learning for community; and learning as community" (p.134).

The Finnish Case

Education has always been an integral part of Finnish culture and society. While access to basic education became a legal obligation and right for all in 1922, Finns have understood that without becoming literate and possessing broad general knowledge, it is difficult to fulfill one's aspirations in life. Teachers, too, gradually assumed these professional leadership responsibilities as the public-school system began expanding in Finland in the early 20th Century. Primarily due to their inherited high social standing, teachers enjoyed great respect and also trust in Finland. Indeed, Finns continue to regard teaching as a noble, prestigious profession - akin to physicians, lawyers, or economists - and driven mainly by moral purpose, rather than by material interests or rewards.

Teachers are the main reason why Finland now leads the international community in literacy, as well as in science and mathematics achievement. Of course, many other factors have contributed to high educational performance. Those educational accomplishments seem all the more remarkable given that Finnish children do not start primary school until age seven. The educational system in Finland today consists of an optional pre-school year at the age of six, followed by nine-year basic school (*peruskoulu*), compulsory to all. In principle, basic school consists of a six-year primary school and a three-year lower secondary school (junior high school). This is followed by a voluntary three-year upper secondary education that has two main optional streams: general (*lukio*) and vocational education (*ammattikoulu*). Both streams lead to higher education, either in a university or polytechnic. Content experts and subject-focused teachers provide instruction in the upper grades of basic school, as well as at general and vocational upper-secondary levels.

Enrollment and completion rates in Finland are, by international comparisons, very high. According to data from Statistics Finland (2009), nearly 98 percent of the six-year-old cohort attend optional pre-school classes, 99 percent complete compulsory basic education (mostly without repeating grades or delays), and 95 percent of basic school graduates immediately continue their studies in the upper secondary school of their choice. Drop-outs from general and vocational upper secondary school (high school) have become rare, declining from high figures in the 1980s. Intensive student counseling and individualized study programs help Finland attain an average 98 percent completion rate among all those who begin general upper-secondary school (Statistics Finland, 2009; Välijärvi & Sahlberg, 2008).

The Finnish Education system has many differences compared to public education in Alberta, or Canada in general. The Finnish system lacks rigorous school inspection, doesn't employ external standardized student testing to inform the public about school performance, and has adopted the idea of promoting social justice as one foundation of education. A National Matriculation Examination at the end of upper secondary education is the only external high-stakes instrument used in Finnish schools. Teacher education is fully congruent with these characteristics of educational policy in Finland.

Finland defines five categories of teachers (Sahlberg, 2011):

(1) *Kindergarten teachers* work in kindergarten classrooms and are also licensed to teach pre-school classes;
(2) *Primary school teachers* teach in grades 1 to 6 of unified nine-year basic schools. They normally are assigned to one grade and teach several subjects;
(3) *Subject teachers* teach specific subjects in the upper grades of basic school (typically grades 7 to 9) and in general upper secondary school, including also vocational schools. Subject teachers may be specialized to teach one to three subjects, e.g. mathematics, physics, and chemistry;
(4) *Special education teachers* work with individuals and groups of students with special needs in primary schools and upper grades of basic schools; and
(5) *Vocational education teachers* teach in upper secondary vocational schools. They must possess at least three years of work experience in their own teaching field before they are admitted to a vocational teacher preparation program.

Teachers and teaching are highly regarded in Finland. The Finnish media regularly report results of opinion polls that document favorite professions among general upper-secondary school graduates. Surprisingly, among young Finns, *teaching* is consistently rated as the most admired profession, leading the ratings of medical doctors, architects and lawyers (*Helsingin Sanomat*, 2004). Teaching is congruent with core social values of Finns: social justice, caring for others, and happiness. Teaching is also regarded as an independent profession that enjoys public respect and praise. It is particularly popular among young women – more than 80 percent of those accepted for study in primary teacher education programs are talented women.

Indeed, teachers are admired individuals in Finnish society. In a national survey, about 1,300 adult Finns (ages 15 to 74) were asked if their spouse's (or partner's) profession has influenced their decision to commit to a relationship with them (*Helsingin Sanomat*, 2008). Interviewees were asked to select five professions from a list of 30 that would be preferred for a selected partner or spouse. The findings were rather surprising. Finnish males viewed a teacher as the most desired spouse, rated just ahead of a nurse, medical doctor, and architect. Women, in turn, admire only a medical doctor and a veterinarian ahead of a teacher as a profession for their ideal husband. In the entire sample, 35 percent rated a teacher as among the top five preferred professions for their ideal spouse. Apparently, only medical doctors are more sought after in Finnish mating markets than are teachers. This clearly documents both the high professional and social status teachers reached in Finland – in and out of schools.

Only Finland's best and brightest are able to fulfill those professional dreams, however. Every spring, thousands of Finnish general upper secondary school graduates submit applications to Departments of Teacher Education in eight Finnish universities, including many of the most talented, creative, and motivated youngsters. Becoming a primary school teacher in Finland is highly competitive. It is normally insufficient to complete general upper secondary school successfully and pass a rigorous Matriculation Examination (an external upper secondary school graduation examination). Successful candidates must also possess the highest scores, positive personalities, and excellent interpersonal skills. Annually, only about one of every 10 of such students will be accepted to prepare to become a teacher in Finnish primary schools. The total annual applicants in all five categories of teacher education programs is about 20,000.

Teacher education is an important and recognized part of higher education in Finland. In many other nations, the situation is different: teacher preparation is frequently viewed as a semi-professional education arranged outside of academic universities. In the Acts on Teacher Education of 1978-79, the minimum requirement for permanent employment as a teacher became a Master's degree that includes an approved Master's thesis with similar scientific requirements as in any other academic field. This legislative policy was the impetus to transfer all teacher education programs from colleges to Finnish universities. The seeds were sown for believing that the teachers' profession is based on scholarly research. An important side-effect of this transition was the unification of the Finnish teaching cadre, which had become divided in the Basic School Reform of 1972. Since the beginning of 1980, all teachers earn Master's degrees and they are all members of the same Teacher Union.

All teachers today, as holders of Master's degrees, are automatically qualified for post-graduate studies. The major subject in the primary school teacher-education program is *education*. In subject-focused teacher education programs, students concentrate in a particular subject, e.g. mathematics or foreign languages. Subject-focused teacher candidates also study didactics, consisting of pedagogical content knowledge within their own subject specialty. There are no alternative ways to receive a teacher's diploma in Finland; the university degree constitutes a license to teach. Successful completion of a Master's degree in teaching today takes, according to the Ministry of Education (2007), on average, from five to seven and half years.

Finnish teacher education focuses on balanced development of the prospective teacher's personal and professional competences, including leadership in and out of the classroom. Particular attention is devoted to building pedagogical thinking skills, enabling teachers to manage instructional processes in accordance with contemporary educational knowledge and practice (Niemi, 2002; Westbury, Hansen, Kansanen, & Björkvist, 2005). In primary teacher education, this is led by the study of education as a main subject, composed of three major thematic areas:

    (a) the theory of education;
    (b) pedagogical content knowledge; and
    (c) subject didactics and practice.

Research-based teacher education programs culminate in a required Master's thesis. Prospective primary school teachers normally complete their theses in the field of education. Subject-focused prospective teachers, in turn, select a topic within their major subject. The level of scholarly expectations for teacher education is similar across all teacher-preparation programs, from elementary to upper secondary school.

Teacher leadership as a distributed craft

Martti is an experienced teacher in a sub-urban primary school in southern Finland. He has a long career as a teacher and also as a principal. He is working in a school of about 350 students and 25 full-time teachers. His school can be considered advanced and modern. It has been actively engaged in several national and local school improvement initiatives. This school is specialized in offering children meaningful and educationally rich after-school activities that Martti says "balance the formal learning with non-formal learning and recreation" and that are seen as an integral part of the work of the school.

As was described earlier, teachers in Finland enjoy social respect and also professional autonomy in their schools. Martti has seen the change from the old and more centrally managed times and thinks that "this is the sign of trust by the education authorities and has forced us here in school to rethink leadership and organization of the entire school". Teachers in his school are both in charge of and responsible for their school curriculum, system, and procedures of student assessment, as well as teaching and learning materials, and even programming of work in each school year. "The Ministry of Education never and the local education authorities rarely intervene in what we do here", says Martti, who also thinks that a high professional level of teacher education has helped teachers to take professional leadership of their own schools.

In his school, Martti experiences what Hargreaves and Fink (2006) have termed "distributed leadership". In fact, this implies that each teacher in school is expected to lead at least some aspects of his or her school. "Our principal", explains Martti, "is in charge of the normal management of school and pedagogical leadership of our staff". This includes curriculum development, assessment and self-evaluation of the school, operational development of after-school activities, and continuous interaction with the local community. This leaves a lot of room for teachers to be in leadership positions. "But this doesn't mean that work or leadership in our school would be fragmented or simply delegated to different teachers", says Martti. He believes that each teacher has voluntarily accepted leadership of certain initiatives in their school.

What does Martti think about the role of distributed leadership in his school? First, it has created a common spirit of "our school and our pupils" in his school. When leading together and sharing responsibilities with each other and their principal, teachers have been able to establish a truly collective culture in their school. Teacher leadership is "a natural way of sharing responsibilities and work together towards a shared goal". Second, it has "raised the level of prestige and sense of professionalism" among teachers. Teacher education provides teachers with basic ideas of teachers as leaders, and it also encourages teacher-students to take ownership of their teaching practice. Dialogue among staff is "much more focused on educational issues and respectful when each teacher is in some way engaged in leadership of the school". Although not all teachers are equally involved in leadership, they all accept that others do so. Third, sharing responsibilities in school has also increased collegiality and interdependency among the staff. Many more teachers than before think that the school can succeed only if everyone does their duties well.

Transforming *accountability* in the Finnish education system into *shared responsibility* among teachers has been one of the culminating ideas in promoting teacher leadership there. The case study of Martti's school is by no means an exception. The OECD review of educational leadership in Finland recognized the widely spread philosophy of distributed leadership in Finnish schools (Hargreaves et al., 2007). Sharing ideas, materials, and even financial resources among schools is not an uncommon thing in Finland. It is noteworthy that most of the distributed leadership examples in Finland are community-generated interventions rather than mandated acts. Schools have a lot of autonomy in municipalities and they can normally decide how leadership on one hand and teachers' work on the other hand are to be organized. Many students in teacher education programs in Finnish universities explain that it is exactly this professional autonomy and teacher leadership in schools that are linked to high prestige and popularity of the teaching profession in Finland.

Sustaining the 'gentle actions' of teacher leaders
What do the Alberta and Finnish cases share?

Trond Undheim (2008), his book, *Leadership from Below*, highlights the need to move away from hierarchical leadership practices; instead recognizing that "nobody is in charge of everything" (p. 16). In today's workplace, we see high degrees of mobility coupled with the fact that the discrete complex skills needed to mobilize purposeful action means that individuals in complex systems often possess skills more advanced than their managers.

The frame for 'leadership from below' originates in Scandinavia with a long tradition of work-life balance, peer leadership, coaching, mentoring, and interdisciplinary teamwork. Project-based management models like self-governed groups were pioneered in Scandinavian companies such as Volvo in the 1980s. These distributed leadership models have their analogue in the technological domain in the experience of Linus Torvalds of Finland, who developed the Linux operating system, and who has inspired a growing use of Open Source principles across the globe.

Using a variety of examples and anecdotes, Undheim illustrates a growing leadership paradigm which takes into account, among other things, our too-often distracted social environment characterized by the unrelenting pace of technological change, workforce and societal diversity and intense competition. As an alternative, Undheim sees a new authentic leadership paradigm focused on being 'present' - continually reminding ourselves that technology and our increasingly brittle social systems mean that "dependency is never far away".

> *While instant communications offer multifarious opportunities for increased efficiency and efficacy, they can become a burden. Regardless of media, it would be best to set limits for its use and follow through. Intel co-founder Andy Grove said, "Only the paranoid survive". However, the opposite may be true, since only the balanced leaders survive (and have families, work-life balance, hobbies, and friends). In fact, technologies have politics - the politics of its designers.*
>
> Undheim, 2008, p. 60

In a symposium sponsored by the Alberta Teachers' Association in 2006, David Peat[3], a world-renowned expert on chaos theory and author of more than 20 books, including ***Blackfoot Physics: A Journey into the Native American Universe***, noted that people need to understand that complex organic systems like modern society can be influenced in positive ways by small but powerfully disruptive "gentle actions", like a stone tossed into a calm pool of water. In the Alberta context, the moral imperatives of leadership that focuses on small but powerful "gentle actions", rather than large-scale plans and grand interventions, can be seen across the province in hundreds of everyday examples.

---

[3] See *Changing Landscapes of the Next Alberta*. Available from the Alberta Teachers' Association. www.ata.ab.ca

Peat's recent 2008 book, *Gentle Action: Bringing Creative Change to a Turbulent World*, continues the conversation by arguing that smaller, community-generated interventions - or "gentle actions" - should be considered before dramatic (often mandated) system-wide programs. He argues that the aggregate of many of these gentle actions working in concert can have a greater impact than a handful of grandiose world-changing projects backed by influential stakeholders.

Peat encourages us all to be more reflective, arguing that people and institutions should think deeply about the inherent limitations and uncertain consequences of any effort to improve a community. He makes the case for individuals and institutions to hold back quick judgment on what it takes to effect positive social change; contending that philanthropists and international organizations should harness the creativity and assets inherent in the communities they wish to serve.

Teacher leadership in the next wave of school renewal efforts will continue to reflect what leadership has always been about: creating possibility where there seem to be only limitations.

> Creativity becomes an important principle at the school level. Teachers who are catalysts of learning in the knowledge society must therefore be provided with incentives and encouraged to make their workplaces, especially classrooms, creative learning environments where openness to new ideas and approaches flourish.

> Finally, risk-taking needs to be encouraged in daily life and learning in schools (Sahlberg, 2010, p. 10).

The two case studies from Alberta and Finland provide compelling examples; resonating with a growing body of research on teacher leadership that speaks to the emergent complexities of collaborative relationships in organizations that thrive through quiet leadership.[4]

In each of the two cases, the emerging forms of teacher leadership parallel the international review of Naylor, Alexandrou, Garsed, and O'Brien (2008), who examined the many formal and informal ways that teachers are drawn into leadership positions and advocacy roles in their schools and teacher organizations. Their initial observations, clustered around four themes, are reflected in many of the experiences reported by teachers, and in the two we illustrated in this paper:

- Leadership roles often evolved naturally and were not planned
- Leadership occurred and evolved when the teachers felt passionately about tasks or approaches that they felt must be completed or addressed
- Leadership was not necessarily recognized, as it was assumed rather than proclaimed
- Credibility among peers was crucial to taking leadership roles.

---

[4] For a full description of quiet leadership see Henry Mintzberg: http://www.processwrite.com/bloghost/manasclerk/archives/2004/12/mintzberg-on-developing-the-developing-world.html

The forms of leadership that emerged in the experiences of these two teachers underscore the reality that 'teacher leadership' cannot be reduced to a simplistic representation. As well, they require systematic and willful support.

Central to the concept of collaborative inquiry in the two examples we draw on is the sustaining of open, non-defensive, dialogue facilitated by teacher leaders[5]. Such dialogue does not happen naturally in schools; it must be intentional and facilitated by internal and external networks of leadership.

Teacher leadership configured as a soulcraft distributed through "gentle actions" is the cultural shift that can be systematically supported in schools and systems. Since evidence-informed practice is the fulcrum point for leveraging improvement in curricular inquiry and teaching practice in general,[6] it is important to consider what a model for systematic support would look like.

---

[5] Piggot, E. (1993). Action research as a professional development tool in higher education. College of Education. Massey University, Palmerston North, NZ.
[6] Joseph Murphy. (2004). Leadership for Literacy. Thousand Oaks: Corwin.

One such model, illustrated below, builds teacher leadership capacity at three levels: the individual, interpersonal and organizational.[7]

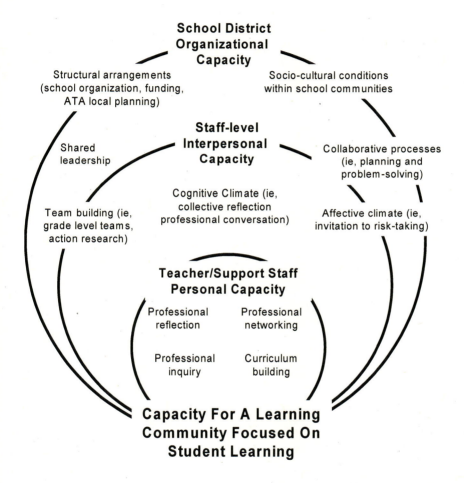

Adapted from Mitchell & Sackney, 2003

---

[7] Adapted from Mitchell, C., & Sackney, L. (2003). Profound improvement: Building capacity for a learning community. Lisse, NL: Swets & Zeitlinger.

For our two exemplars, Kelly and Martti, the following features describe the distributed soulcraft of their work and suggest how the three capacities described above could synergistically interact:

- Clearly defined shared goals emerge for improving student learning
- A supportive climate for collaborative inquiry and risk-taking is fostered
- Leadership sustained by focally real 'gentle actions'.

These features are in keeping with Bush & Glover's, perception of "deep learning" for teachers where:

> Deep learning is centred on the creation of personal understanding through reflection (individual and shared) which results in the creation of knowledge, which can then be transformed into action.[8]

Conclusion

As more countries grant greater autonomy to schools in designing curricula and managing resources to raise achievement, the role of the school leader has grown far beyond that of administrator. Developing school leaders requires clearly

---

[8] Bush, T. & Glover, D. (2003). Leadership Development for New School Leaders: The New Visions Induction to Headship Programme. Paper presented at BELMAS Conference, Milton Keynes, October.

defining their responsibilities, providing access to appropriate professional development throughout their careers, and acknowledging their pivotal roles and responsibilities...

Andreas Schleicher, 2012, p. 13

If teacher leadership is to be scaled-out as an intentional aspect of the work of school improvement, then educational policy internationally ought to identify the ways that it might be supported and sustained as a form of *soulcraft* in the form of "gentle actions". This might become a way of imagining 'professional responsibility' in the context of seeing teachers' work as a practical wisdom brought to the daily encounters with students, the curriculum and the community.

The focal practices undertaken by Kelly and Martti represent a particularly rich expression of the democratic nature of collaborative inquiry in ethically driven school communities. The two teacher-leaders described in this chapter were caught up in the "the very particularity of the obligation to the other" and in the difficulties of what Barber (1995) calls the localized places of our "common living" such as our homes, workplace and public spaces. The moral commitment to both the students and to each other as colleagues drove the focally real practices of these two teacher leaders.

We need school- and system-level support structures that foster and enable teacher ingenuity. The paradox facing school leaders is that 'economic competitiveness' needs to be defined broadly, and must include the contributions of members of society and civic engagement. While business community leaders call for economic competitiveness, creativity and ingenuity (left side of the triangle), governments (including Alberta) have pushed an educational policy emphasizing standardization and narrowly defined outcomes (right side of the triangle) while focusing on results that can be easily measured through large-scale testing programs. The following diagram illustrates the predictable result - a contradiction between what is measured and what is valued in and out of the system:

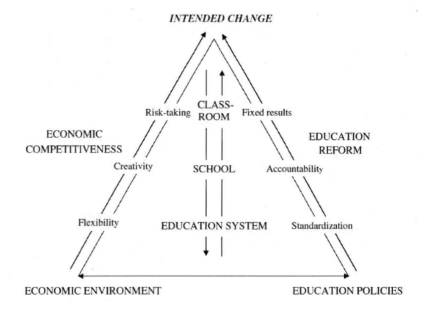

Reg Weaver, President of the National Educational Association, described his mandate as the leader of that organization of three million teachers quite simply, yet evocatively as, "helping teachers helping kids *just to be possible*". [Emphasis is ours.]

Rethinking teacher leadership for the transformation of the education sectors in Alberta and Finland could do no better than to strive for this moral imperative.

References

Barber, B. (1995). *Jihad vs. McWorld*. New York: Random House.

Borgmann, A. (1992). *Crossing the Postmodern Divide*. London: University of Chicago Press.Crawford, Michael. (2009). *From Shop Class to Soulcraft – An Inquiry into the Value of Work*. New York: Penguin.

Hargreaves, A.; Crocker, R.; Davis, B.; McEwen, L.; Sahlberg, P.; Sumara D.; Shirley, D.; and Hughes, M. (2009). *The Learning Mosaic: A multiple perspectives review of the Alberta*. Edmonton, Alberta: Alberta Education.Hargreaves, A., Fink, D. (2006). Sustainable Leadership. San Francisco, CA: Jossey-Bass.

Hargreaves, A.; Halasz, G.; and Pont, B. (2007). *School Leadership for Systemic Improvement in Finland*. A Case Study Report for the OECD Activity "Improving School Leadership". Paris: OECD.

Harris, Alma. (Ed.) 2009. *Distributed Leadership*. Scranton: Springer. Helsingin Sanomat. (2004). *Ykkössuosikki: Opettajan Ammatti* [Top favorite: Teaching Profession]. February 11, 2004.

Helsingin Sanomat (2008). *Millä Ammatilla Pääsee Naimisiin?* [Which profession to get married?] Koulutusliite, 27 February.

Helsinki, 4-6. Retrieved from
http://www.lulu.com/content/2061825

Alberta Initiative for School Improvement. (2009). Edmonton: Alberta Education. Retrieved from http://education.alberta.ca/admin/aisi.aspxMascall, B. &

Leithwood, K. (2008). Leaders Working Within Teacher Unions: Can networks build understanding and capacity? *Educational Administration Quarterly, 44*(4), 529-561.

Mascall, B.; Leithwood, Kenneth; Strauss. T.; Sacks, R. (2008). The relationship between distributed leadership and teachers' academic optimism. *Journal of Educational Administration(46)*2 214-228.

Ministry of Education (2007). *Opettajankoulutus 2020* [Teacher Education 2020]. Committee Report 2007:44. Helsinki: Ministry of Education.

Naylor, C.; Alexandrou, A.; Garsed, J.; and O'Brien, J. (2008). *An Emerging View of Teacher Leaders Working Within Teacher Unions: Can networks build understanding and capacity?* Paper presented at the American Educational Research Association Annual Conference, 24-28 March.

Niemi, H. (2002). Active Learning: A cultural change needed in teacher education and in schools. *Teaching and Teacher Education 18*(7), 763-780.

Peat, D. (2008). *Gentle Action: Bringing creative change to a turbulent world*. Pari, Italy: Pari Press.

Sahlberg, P. (2008). *Learning First*. Paper presented at the Leadership in Educational Accountability Conference in Edmonton, April 18 to 19, 2008.

Sahlberg, P. (2010, forthcoming). The Most Wanted: Teachers and teacher education in Finland. In L. Darling-Hammond & A. Lieberman (Eds.) *International Teacher Education: Practices & Policies in High Achieving Nations*. New York: Routledge.

Sahlberg, P.; and Oldroyd, D. (2010). Pedagogy for economic competitiveness and sustainable development. *European Journal of Education*, 45(2), pages not available. Sahlberg, P (2011) *Finnish Lessons – What the World Can Learn from Educational Change in Finland*. New York: Teachers College Press.

Schleicher, A. 2012. *Preparing Teachers and Developing School Leaders for the 21st Century*. New York: OECD. http://www.oecd.org/dataoecd/4/35/49850576.pdf

Statistics Finland. (2009). *Education*. Retrieved from http://www.stat.fi/til/kou_en.html.

Stoll, L.; Fink, D. and Earl. L. 2003. *It's About Learning (and It's About Time)*. London: Routledge Falmer.

Undheim, Todd. (2008). *Leadership from Below*. New York: Lulu.com. Retrieved fromhttp://www.leadershipfrombelow.com/

Välijärvi, J. & Sahlberg, P. (2008). Should a 'failing' student repeat a grade? Retrospective response from Finland. *Journal of Educational Change*, 9(4), 385-389.Westbury, I..; Hansen, S-E.;Kansanen, P.; & Björkvist, O. (2005). Teacher education for research-based practice in expanded roles: Finland's experience. *Scandinavian Journal of Educational Research, 49*(5), 475-485.

Teacher Leadership in Navigating the Multiple Spaces that Support Inclusion

C. (Charlie) Naylor

> *Teacher leadership can take many forms. Teacher leaders show themselves in many ways both in and out of school. Not all teacher leaders are visible. Some do their job quietly and without fanfare. They focus on their students. They respect their peers. They recognize that diversity within the teaching profession is good. They are willing to accept change and work with it. They are constantly looking for ways to improve themselves, their classrooms, and their schools. They are patient and try to maintain their perspective, taking into account the "big picture." They accept the use of technology as an essential tool for instruction and productivity. They are not threatened by people who are more outgoing and extroverted than themselves. They actively try to get parents involved in school life. Teacher leaders inspire the people around them.*
>
> *Hess, R.T. (2008) Follow the Teacher: Making a Difference for School Improvement.*
> *Lanham: Rowman & Littlefield Education.*

Introduction

In recent years, there has been increasing interest in leadership development that supports and nurtures teachers to develop a broad range of leadership capacities. This debate has gone hand in hand with an increasing interest in the notion of distributed leadership. Distributed leadership takes many forms, but arguably has two defining features: First, that leadership is decentralized i.e. the capacity to lead is undertaken by a broader range of individuals, many of whom may be considered to be at junior levels within their organization. Second, that the type of leadership being exercised is more fluid and informal. It depends less on formal authority (based on traditional sources of power and status), and more on informal leadership and the use of influence (the capacity to bring about change, without necessarily having formal authority).

The above quote and brief introduction to distributed forms of leadership reflect perspectives on teacher leadership that are closest to the views of leadership preferred within teacher unions - a teacher leader not focused on hierarchy, but on students or peers, and working with an acceptance of change and technology while actively building relationships with parents. It's a leadership of ideas and action, not one of status and ego. This, and other approaches to teacher leadership, have been one focus of the British Columbia Teachers' Federation's (BCTF) Research Department in recent years. These approaches have been documented in the BCTF's 'Teacher and Educational Leadership' web page,[9] which includes details of an international collaborative research project to examine teacher leadership, as

---

[9] See http://bctf.ca/IssuesInEducation.aspx?id=22473

well as analyses of the literature and various links to other sources of teacher leadership research.

While the issue of teacher leadership is of general interest within teacher unions, this paper explores a more specific focus within the leadership theme - that of teacher leadership to support *inclusion*. Five areas of the BCTF's focus will be considered, all of which have taken place in the last ten years:

1. Mentorship for teachers new to special education
2. The 'Teaching to Diversity' web page
3. The Richmond Inclusion Review
4. Teacher inquiry to support inclusive approaches
5. Addressing students' mental health issues

Mentoring for Teachers New to Special Education

The project was initiated and based on findings from the BCTF's research project, which examined the current status of inclusive education in two school districts in 2002.[10] After the B.C. Liberal government stripped contract provisions in 2002 (which had provided ratios of special education teachers) there were large reductions in staffing those positions. In addition, many experienced special education and learning assistance teachers left their roles for classroom positions when their caseloads and workloads increased beyond what they considered manageable. As a result, special education and learning assistance became an

---

[10] See http://bctf.ca/IssuesInEducation.aspx?id=5794

entry-level job in many B.C. school districts, with new teachers and teachers new to the role struggling to support the needs of both classroom teachers and of students with special needs.

The intention was to provide one approach to support the needs of teachers new to the special education/learning assistance roles with a group process accessing the knowledge of peers and facilitated by experienced special education/learning assistance teachers.

Three school districts were involved: Nanaimo, Coquitlam, and Prince George. The project was a BCTF/local teacher association/school district collaboration. The collaborative nature of this project was crucial. In each district, the local teacher association and school district staff supported it with funds, endorsement, and participation in planning and ongoing dialogue to support and manage the project in each school. One key element was that each initiative fit within local priorities as agreed by the local teacher association and the school district. Thus each project becomes less of an "add-on" than a part of what each district might be addressing in the school year. The BCTF also provides some funds and staff time to support planning, implementing, and documenting the projects.

A key feature of this project was teacher leadership. Mentoring was based on a group process, with two teacher-leaders facilitating groups of 12–15 teachers. This reflects a view of mentorship very different to the one-on-one favoured in much of the literature. The group process combined job-specific expertise with a mastery of facilitation processes in the function of the two teacher-leader facilitators. It was leadership based on role-specific professional knowledge, and building on facilitation skills inherent in many teachers but honed with additional training provided by the union. In addition, there was an explicit acknowledgement of expertise within the group, and acceptance that those being mentored also had knowledge, skills, and actual or potential leadership capacity.

We believe there is evidence that a three-way collaboration (provincial/local teacher union and school district) of this kind has the potential to build more sustainable projects, because each partner offers supports which complement the efforts of the other partners. It also helps that each partner has identified the focus as a priority, and that there exists agreement between parties on such priorities. A more detailed exploration of the mentoring project can be found on the BCTF web site[11]. For information regarding other aspects of the union's approach to collaboration, read the paper, *"A teacher union's collaborative research agenda and strategies: One way forward for Canadian teacher unions in supporting teachers' Professional Development."*[12]

The BCTF provided: initial training in mentoring; some release time; staff time and support; videoconference facilities and

---

[11] http://bctf.ca/IssuesInEducation.aspx?id=14026
[12] See http://www.bctf.ca/uploadedFiles/Publications/Research_reports/2005tr01.pdf

discussion; end-of-year evaluation; and online publication of project reports. The school districts' contributions also supported some release time. Training sessions were held at the BCTF for teachers who were to facilitate the mentoring/professional conversation groups. A variety of approaches to release time were used. In most cases, teachers met for three of the meetings in school time, with substitute teachers provided, and met three times out of school time, with a dinner provided. BCTF staff initiated the project, liaised with each district's facilitators, visited sites during the year and provided initial training in mentorship/professional conversation approaches.

Videoconferencing facilities had been established by the BCTF in Vancouver, Prince George, and Nanaimo. All three sites (with Coquitlam mentors participating at the BCTF offices) were connected for videoconferences. This enabled each site to share their approach and to discuss issues. The discussion provided data for evaluation, and reflection—one such reflection is shared below:

> *One key finding from this project is that teachers are leaders but in order to lead effectively they need encouragement and support. Our experience is that these are best provided within a community of peers where we all learn from each other and at times we may each take on leadership role, so that strengths in facilitation, technology, the specialist teacher's role, etc. are all recognized wherever they exist within the group and utilized as and when needed.*

While the mentoring approach developed to support special education and learning assistance teachers is not operational at this time, many of its processes are being utilized in both union and districts' efforts to support teacher inquiry in projects across the province. Thus, while 'programs' have a limited shelf life, they can leave a legacy in terms of improved processes, facilitation skills and collaboration that might still positively contribute to the further development of teachers' professional learning.

The 'Teaching to Diversity' Web Page

The development of this web page reflects the teacher leadership demonstrated by three Provincial Specialist Associations (PSAs) of the BCTF. There are 33 PSAs, some subject-focused (math, social studies, etc.), others role-specific (special education) or linked to teaching specific ranges of students (primary, intermediate). Most host web sites and publish journals, offering teacher leadership with a professional focus in role or subject across a wide range of teachers' work and interests.

The teacher-leaders in three PSAs (special education, learning assistance, and ESL) developed the web page with the BCTF research staff in order to provide better access for teachers to resources linked to inclusion. It allows for a 'one-stop-shop' to access resources such as ministry policies, professional development opportunities, student transitions and differentiated instruction/universal design. Its resources are selected by teachers for teachers, and for several years the BCTF supported teachers - offering introductory sessions for teachers in many school districts so that they would become more familiar with the site and its contents.

Some innovative features of this web page include:

- **A glossary of terms:**[13] This extensive glossary enables site visitors to access definitions of terms and often provides links to further information. This was produced because many teachers new to the role or the profession were having difficulty understanding terms in common usage with more experienced teachers.
- **A professional development section:**[14] Teachers can find current workshop and conference offerings within B.C., as

---

[13] See http://www.bctf.ca/issues/resources.aspx?id=10572

[14] See http://www.bctf.ca/IssuesInEducation.aspx?id=10596

well as on-line PD. There is also access to a submission process where teachers may submit (on-line) a short description of their upcoming PD session to the BCTF staff, who then posts it in the "Upcoming Events" section of the PD page.

Teacher leadership in this case reflects a form of service, not only to the wider membership of the union, but also to anyone in the community who might have an interest in inclusive approaches that supports all learners' needs. It shows how teacher-leaders can develop a collaborative approach across their own associations, but within the union build a product of utility to their peers, to others employed in the education system and to parents and the community. The web page is currently being reviewed and updated with new information related to areas such as universal design and students' mental health issues.

The Richmond Inclusion Review Action Plan, 2008- Present
Richmond is a school district in the metropolitan area of Vancouver. A consultant's report concluded the first phase of the district's review, which was guided by a committee including union and parent representation. The Richmond Teachers' Association (RTA), a local of the BCTF, developed an application submitted to the BCTF for a teacher inquiry grant to involve teachers after the report was published. It proposed establishing a teacher inquiry group with the following mandate.

> The group will consider the report and identify possible directions in terms of:

- extending the discussion about inclusion in schools and society
- advocating for increased support and resources
- exploring areas of and approaches to professional development
- accessing resources and information from existing sources
- networking within the district and provincially to access resources and professional development
- sharing information through the use of technology
- considering the potential role of community organizations in supporting K-12 Inclusion[15]

The application was funded by the BCTF with matching funds provided by the Richmond School District. The proposal reflects teacher leadership from a teacher local where the union is encouraging its members to participate in professional learning experiences which extend thinking about and acting to support inclusion. But by moving within an inquiry approach, the teacher association also encouraged a form of autonomous and self-directed professional development which reflects teacher leadership; in part because of its use of teachers as facilitators. Teacher inquiry was articulated in a BCTF report[16] as follows.

---

[15] RTA submission for a BCTF teacher inquiry grant, 2008
[16] http://www.bctf.ca/uploadedFiles/Public/Publications/TeacherInquirer/archive/2008-02/BCTFTeacherInquiryWGReport2008.pdf

Teacher inquiry is a process that involves:

- Reflection on practice
- Collaboration
- Professional conversation—accessing our own knowledge and the knowledge of peers
- Moving out of individual and isolated space to collective and public space
- Extending understanding of practice through critical discourse
- Planning and initiating some form of action for change
- Distributed leadership.

Teacher inquiry as developed by the BCTF includes the following principles:

- It taps into teachers' lived experience
- It includes "unboundaried," open questions (i.e., whatever questions participants bring)
- It involves an inquiring group of colleagues
- It invites and encourages reciprocal learning
- It is run by teachers, for teachers.

One approach utilized in the first phase of inquiry involved the encouraging of school-based conversations on the issue of inclusive education. In encouraging such conversations, it was felt that teams of facilitators would effectively and efficiently facilitate the conversations. A one-day training session for these potential facilitators was developed by union staff with some expertise in the area. The inquiry was jointly funded by the BCTF and the school district, and school district staff participated in both the planning and the running of facilitation training for school-based conversations. Thus, teacher leadership was utilized and extended but within a collaboration with school district management. Collaborations between unions and school districts often involve union and district staff, as representatives, agreeing to a program. But this collaboration involves the union participants as knowledgeable and skilled in terms of processes such as facilitation and inquiry, thereby using the capacity of the union to implement inquiry and its processes rather than just to organize it.

Another part of the action plan involved teachers describing and sharing 'promising practices.' For some of this work, teachers are experimenting with a range of communication approaches, including video, graphic organizers, and Web 2.0 technologies. Video is used to share interviews where teachers describe some of the approaches used, with graphic organizers and other methods used to share information about practice which is easily accessible to teachers. The quality of much of the video is somewhat basic, yet we have found this encourages access rather than deterring it. Other teachers have commented that the technical limitations of the video make it more real (more like schools) than a slick and professionally produced video that might project more style than substance.

So there are two major parts to this leadership: that of teachers reflecting publicly on their practice; and that of teachers leading some of the processes that allow for such reflections and sharing. By reflecting publicly, such teachers are offering ideas on what they think works well. To do so requires some courage and a measure of humility (two qualities of leadership by example), an implicit recognition of imperfection and a trust in peers to engage positively and constructively. Teachers facilitating processes of reflection are utilizing skills they have developed in the service of the profession, so that teachers can engage in conversations and discourse within processes that are effective and time-efficient.

Teacher Inquiry to Support Inclusive Approaches: Special Education Association's exploration of differentiated instruction, 2008

The BCTF's support for teacher inquiry has, to date, included offering two grants each year to the BCTF's PSAs. In one project, the Special Education Association (SEA) was funded to explore the concept of differentiated instruction. A group of SEA members met for five half-day sessions with a BCTF facilitator. The general focus question for the group inquiry was:

> *How can special educators work together with classroom teachers in the identification and application of critical elements of differentiated*

instruction in order to ensure success for every student?

Within this 'umbrella theme', each of the SEA group members conducted an individual investigative inquiry/action research project emerging from their specific interest and teaching practice.

Individual questions:
- *Does the use of student information about a student's style, interests, and readiness for learning during the Individual Educational Planning (IEP) process lead to greater success and happiness for a student with special needs?*
- *Do French immersion teachers agree that the use of leveled books, as an aspect of differentiated instruction in a second language classroom, leads to increased decoding and comprehension skills?*
- *How does inquiry engage classroom teachers to use DI strategies?*
- *How do you promote DI as being manageable for classroom teachers?*
- *How do you assist teachers to become familiar with DI and to implement DI in their classrooms? What are some entry points?*
- *What are some of the effective ways support staff can work with a classroom teacher to provide differentiated learning for students?*

Thus, the group's focus on individual areas of practice was combined with the 'umbrella theme' to allow for consideration of the teachers' own work in the context of differentiating instruction. One aspect of the inquiry process is that participants choose which way to share their journey of learning and their findings with a wider audience and this group decided on the development of a Wiki.

Reflecting on the experience, a representative of the group wrote:

> *The collegial dialogue during our focused time together was very valuable for all participants. As well, the time away was spent reflecting and extending our thinking. The challenge of having the participants from all over British Columbia was resolved by creating a wiki as a depository for all of our reflections, ideas, and resources. This challenge led us to a solution for sharing resources in the time in between when we met and became a valuable resource as the outcome. The wiki then became a legacy for others to share our work.*
>
> *Another success was the focus on students and how they can be more successful, so more and more students in British Columbia who had been struggling, now had new opportunities to demonstrate their knowledge in many different ways. Student engagement in learning increased. As well, students felt understood and the information used was, in some cases, shared during the IEP process which was helpful for goal development and parents felt that their children were more fully supported.*

Wikis are either open to anyone or accessible by invitation. The Wiki space developed and shared by the group was initially by invitation and then (once the Wiki was as complete as time allowed during the inquiry) open to anyone. In some interesting ways, this evolution mirrors the process of the union's inquiry groups. By moving into an inquiry group, an individual teacher moves out of the 'private' space of a classroom into a 'public' (yet to some extent sheltered) space of an inquiry group. By moving from the private space of the 'invite-only' Wiki to a space where anyone can access the information on a public Wiki, the group moved beyond its own safe space and into a forum where its work could be viewed, extended or challenged. In the same way, all BCTF inquiry groups are required to share their journey of learning with wider audiences, thereby going more 'public' with their learning, and also opening them up to debate and challenge.

The Wiki reflects a product of inquiry, whereas much of the benefit of inquiry is linked to the processes involved—in particular the exploration of questions and ideas over time and in collaboration and dialogue with peers. The 'process-product' argument has raged for decades, but I would argue that both are important components of inquiry. Without careful facilitation of process, inquiry often fails. And within the inquiry process, the conversations and dialogue that take place enhance and extend participants' understanding of practice in ways that are hard to identify as 'product'.

Yet at the same time, the inquiry approach is funded and some 'product' is required. This might be the recounting of the journey of learning, a description of a changed practice, or an illustration of changed understanding in pedagogy or role.

Wikis have been used in the BCTF's inquiry approaches for:

- managing a project
- accessing information for participants
- reporting on a project
- democratizing communication in inquiry
- accessing the 'spaces' between meetings.

Wikis and other Web 2.0 technologies are tools which are increasingly being utilized to support inquiry processes and reporting. In the SEA's inquiry, it was used as a dissemination tool so that other teachers could access information on differentiated instruction and learn from the experiences of the inquiry group. Thus, with a focus on individual areas of inquiry within an 'umbrella' theme of differentiation, participants both followed their own areas of focus and prepared and published a resource for their peers.

Addressing Students' Mental Health Issues

Inclusion is a philosophy which articulates the ideal that all students belong in schools that are intended to meet their academic and social needs. One challenge—the mental health of students—is growing in prominence in Canada, as well as in a number of other countries and leads to negative personal and educational outcomes:

Unrecognized and untreated mental disorders can lead to a variety of negative long- and short-term outcomes, such as poor educational and vocational achievement, problematic social and personal functioning, and reduced life expectancy due to associated medical conditions and suicide.

Bhatia, 2007; Kessler, Foster, Saunders, & Stang, 1995

Mental disorders can also negatively affect young people through their impact on learning. For example, mental disorders may lead to chronic absenteeism or early school leaving.

McEwan, Waddell, & Barker, 2007; Saluja et al., 2009[17]

Mental health disorders in children and youth hinder inclusion. They do so because students with a range of disorders from anxiety and depression to self-harm and potential suicide often find themselves outside mainstream participation in schools.

While some progress has been made in supporting inclusive education for many students with disabilities, the same cannot be said for supporting students with mental health issues. The lack of awareness may be so pervasive that some curriculum likely triggers issues, such as eating disorders in some students—when, for instance, there are lessons or discussions of body image and health education linked to weight and diet.

---

[17] Comprehensive School Mental Health: An Integrated "School-Based Pathway to Care" Model for Canadian Secondary Schools. (2011) Wei, Y., Kutcher, S. Szumilas, M. *Mc Gill Journal of Education* (46, 2)

Teacher-leaders have emerged in B.C. to address this issue. While being cautious about increasing teacher workload and responsibility, and stressing the distinction between the roles of teachers and health professionals, some cautious steps have been taken to contribute to initiatives that may improve teachers' abilities to both increase awareness of and consider constructive reactions to issues and incidents of students' mental health.

These steps include:

- Two 2011 Provincial Specialist Association conferences (counselors and learning assistance teachers) focusing on mental health of students.
- Participation in an informal network, "The Mental Health Collaboration," which has evolved into a group of approximately 30 people who work in schools, ministries, universities, research centres, or who are parent advocates with knowledge of and interest in students' mental health. This group has accessed Canadian and other resources on its Wiki and is currently developing an action plan to support awareness and appropriate action strategies such as referrals.
- The addition of a mental health page[18] to the BCTF 'Teaching to Diversity' with links to recognized resources such as the B.C. Children's Hospital's Kelty Centre.[19]
- Participation in the planning and operation of two Summer Institutes at the B.C. Children's Hospital[20] for

---

[18] http://www.bctf.ca/issues/resources.aspx?id=24017
[19] http://keltymentalhealth.ca/

teachers and others with a focus on several areas of children's mental health.

While these may be small steps and 'early days,' teacher leadership in this area contributes to collaborative approaches in part by facilitating the links between health care professionals and educators, and by introducing some discussion and a range of resources to teachers. Both areas are more complex than they may appear at first sight. Education–health connections have not always proved easy or successful, and some initial discussions within the Mental Health Collaboration, while not directly facilitating connections in schools, may be an important precursor so that awareness may be improved prior to any potential collaboration.

The issue of mental health information and resources of utility to teachers raises questions of how to gauge and prioritize resources, and how to build teachers' awareness while not encouraging diagnoses or actions which require specialist health professional expertise. In some ways, the greatest benefit may be a better awareness of mental health issues by educators and a better knowledge of the education system for health care professionals, so that positive and successful collaborations may be feasible in the future.

---

[20] http://keltymentalhealth.ca/event/2011/08/summer-institute-2011-promoting-mental-health-bc-schools

Conclusion

These examples reflect a range of activities in which teachers offer leadership to support the needs of all students in B.C.'s schools. Through inquiry, teachers seek to better understand practices that might support inclusion. In mentorship, they use skills and strategies to support teachers new to teaching and/or new to the role of specialist support for inclusion. By building and maintaining a web page, they find and disseminate inclusive information and resources. In both the Richmond Inclusion Review and the Mental Health Collaboration, they connect and work with others within and outside the union to improve approaches, often using graphics, video, and a range of Web 2.0 technologies, including Wikis and on-line conferencing, to communicate with peers and partners and to disseminate learning and resources.

One key learning we have made is that teacher-leaders supporting inclusion are "system navigators," skillfully 'navigating' tides and currents within organizational systems. The term "system navigator" emerged from analysis of qualitative data in our teacher leadership research. Such data showed teacher-leaders working in dual organizations and cultures, union and school district. Union culture in B.C. is far from monolithic because local and provincial cultures vary. Within a local and school district, there may be consistent cultures and relationships over time, or intermittent waves of collaboration or conflict, and varying levels of trust between union and management. Within the union, there are also ranges of perspectives on issues among the local teacher associations. To navigate within the union, therefore, requires knowledge of local and provincial union contexts, factions, and philosophies. It also requires keeping abreast of union initiatives and actions, all of which have been achieved by these effective teacher-leaders.

The approaches to teacher leadership outlined in this paper reflect leadership as service to others and to the profession. There's a considerable modesty and even humility in teacher-leaders who stress supports for students and peers, and engage in collaboration. By working collaboratively, they seek out the knowledge of others, ceding leadership when other expertise surfaces, regaining it when asked, or to ensure progress in the tasks of the group. Their work reflects approaches to leadership where goals are more important than status, and where community values and professional norms of collaboration and respect enable leadership but do not encourage leaders to dominate or control. While we understand more about teacher leadership than we did a few years ago, there is much yet to learn in building and sustaining teacher leadership within a teacher union. We need, therefore, to take what we have done and learned as a base for future learning, and to share our thinking with others across Canada and internationally, while also learning from those who also build and support leadership in teachers.

Teacher Leadership in Action: Prospects and Perils?

Jim Parsons, Christine Stobart, Bobbi Compton, Melissa Humby, and Raime Drake

During the summer of 2010, the University of Alberta Faculty of Education and the Alberta Teachers' Association joined to teach a course on the topic of teacher leadership (August 9-13, at the Alberta Teachers' Association in Edmonton). This 3-credit graduate level course in teacher leadership was based in part on the foundational work of the Alberta Initiative for School Improvement (AISI), and its impact on grassroots school leadership. The course title was *EDSE 501: Teacher Leadership in School Improvement*.

It was co-taught by Jim Parsons, Professor, Faculty of Education, University of Alberta (and one of the authors of this chapter); Kelly Harding, doctoral student in the Department of Secondary Education and school leader at Edmonton Public School Board's Centre High School; J-C Couture, Adjunct Professor and Executive Staff Officer, Alberta Teachers' Association; and Phil McRae, Adjunct Professor and Executive Staff Officer, Alberta Teachers' Association. Thanks to the unique partnership with the Alberta Teachers' Association, guest instructors included Pasi Sahlberg, Director General of Centre for International Mobility in Helsinki, Finland; Dennis Shirley, Professor of Education at Boston College; and Stephen Murgatroyd, former Executive Director External Relations at Athabasca University.

The course was offered as an intense weeklong institute. Graduate students were given pre-session assignments (course readings) and post-session assignments (the completion of an extensive group-designed project to be conducted at the site of their teaching). Twenty-four professional teachers enrolled in this post-graduate class. The course was intense, and students met both during the day and at the end of each day for suppers, talks, and presentations. During the course, graduate students worked together with colleagues and faculty to create the grounded practice project proposal for the work that they would complete over the course of their next year. Given busy schedules, faculty worked to keep up with these graduate students during the year.

During the following year, as I (Jim) traveled to schools throughout the province, I would stop at schools and have coffee or lunch with graduate students who were part of the course. Over the course of the 2010-2011 school year, graduate students were encouraged to complete these projects. There was an expectation that graduate students, who were also teachers, would come together toward the end of the year to confer and share their findings, and the impacts of their projects.

However, even great ideas don't always work as planned. In truth, we cannot say that the follow-up year worked well. Given the realities of classroom and personal life, time became a factor for project completion, and schedules intervened to create difficulties for graduate students/teachers to complete their projects at their sites. Life happens to teachers. Some were moved from one school to another; AISI project funding was stopped;

personal lives became busy; some teachers did not fully complete the projects when the course was completed and grades had been granted; not all teachers were visited. Also, in truth, the course was poorly structured. In retrospect, the course designers should have created one course (offered during the summer) to create the project proposals, and one course (offered throughout the year, with more expectation of close supervision) to complete the project.

This confession aside, several projects were finalized and, as a result, schools and students were impacted in edifying ways. Project successes also included the leadership growth that teachers experienced as they fulfilled their leadership projects. As a course follow-up, course faculty contacted graduate students from the course seeking volunteers to work on a report that would highlight the project work they had completed. Of the 24 graduate students/teachers, four were chosen to work collectively on this; writing a report of about 1000 words reviewing each of the individual projects. These edited reviews make up the body of this chapter.

The reviews were written to follow a simple template consisting of three questions:

1. Proposed Project (What was the project? What did it intend to accomplish?)
2. Project Summary (How was the project enacted? How did it work? Who benefited?)
3. Project Learning (What did you learn from the project?)

These reviews were synthesized and edited for this chapter. The course and the follow-up projects affirm what we have learned over the past eleven years of AISI and in previous research with instructional leadership in Alberta. Teachers are ready and able to work constructively as school leaders. Students and schools benefit when teachers accept and build their leadership capabilities.

Specifically, the papers offer a beginning insight into the possibilities that can emerge when teachers lead educational change and improvement. Teachers' grounded insights (even in this small sample) have accomplished much in the lives of students, parents, and other teachers. We can only imagine what educational growth might occur as teachers come to assume more leadership opportunities across Alberta.

We have also learned that teacher leadership might be supported by wisely creating spaces where teachers can discuss and plan positive changes that impact their sites, students, and schools. Teacher leadership in Alberta is a positive and ground-breaking reality. This graduate course was a pilot, and the papers that emerged helped us learn that teachers, on their own, will seize the day to create positive changes. We also have begun to learn ways to support teachers in their growth. In speaking to teachers who were part of that initial one-week, intense course, they, without exception, lauded the experience – they met and worked with great people, they were inspired by experienced leaders who allowed them to explore their own opportunities for change in the mirror of their experienced learning.

We found teachers committed to leadership projects. And, while they *can* do it alone, building support networks does help. With the involvement of other people, teacher leadership can become an emerging possibility.

Project I. Bridging Theory and Practice for Pre-service Teachers (Christine Stobart is currently a doctoral student at the University of Calgary)

My project was based on a praxis issue I perceived in the pre-service teacher practicum program at the University of Alberta. Student teachers were perplexed and mentor teachers confused by the pedagogical differences they perceived existed between what was taught at the university (theory) and what was modeled and/or expected in the classroom (practice). The two simply did not match. Other university facilitators felt the same. Often, both parties were frustrated by supposed discrepancies, and I believed these needed to be addressed through dialogue that involved the university. As a university facilitator, I believed I could initiate interventions that allowed all constituents to share common understandings of the theory promoted at the university, *and* the practices demonstrated and desired in the classroom. In this way, student teachers would have an enriching and rewarding practicum, and ultimately, students would benefit from consistent teaching.

During the practicum, both student teachers and mentor teachers feel overwhelmed. Because orchestrating meetings between student teachers, mentor teachers, and university facilitators is unfeasible, it seemed that technology might be a viable alternative. Because mandatory daily reflective professional journals are a course requirement, and both mentor teachers and university facilitators comment on the student teacher entries, this forum also seemed fruitful. I believed reflective journals could become blog entries where student and mentor teachers, as well as university facilitators, could all comment on postings regularly, as opposed to the occasional paper versions. Such technology could provide a running conversation with richer dialogue and might alleviate some confusion between theory and practice.

In the first term of the course, I proposed the optional blog idea to all 15 of my student teachers. There were no takers. I believed student teachers, already digital natives, would opt for the chance. However, they seemed reluctant. Despite cajoling, no online journals occurred first term. The second term I was more deliberate. I specifically asked likely pairs of student/mentor teachers if they would participate. Consequently, two pairs agreed. Unfortunately, one willing student teacher quickly realized that teaching wasn't their calling and withdrew. The second pair completed the term and considered the experience a success although, from my point of view, dialogue remained superficial and didn't broach the issues of theory/practice I had hoped for. They liked the format because "it saved paper!" The second term, I mentioned at a university facilitators meeting that I was trying the blog approach to increase dialogue, and received positive nods from peers but little else. I assumed the implementation of technology offered little appeal to the group, because many shared the view that they were "digital immigrants"– just learning technology by use rather than having developed the skills of being a digital native.

To better assess my project, I implemented Schein's conceptual model for managed culture change[21] based on five principles for creating conditions for innovation (Schein, 2010). The application is rudimentary, but helps effectively identify the flaw in the change I initiated. As a university facilitator, I could see that 'survival anxiety' was evident, and I was aware that pre-service teachers cited discrepancies with their mentor teachers in regard to pedagogy. Mentor teachers also noted inadequacies present in student teachers and the program. What I saw for a period of time as whining (suppression) became substantially more disconfirming.

This data highlighted an underlying lack of collaboration between parties. The university taught education theory; mentor teachers taught education practice; and student teachers attempted to synthesize this information. This initial stage of 'unfreezing' my 'survival anxiety' manifested itself in both guilt and frustration, and generated 'learning anxiety' (Principle 1) that eventually forced me to approach my supervisor suggesting an operational change (Principle 2). The operational change, based on a need for more collaboration, focused on implementing online reflective journals all parties could access (Principle 3). Most student teachers were indifferent to this proposed change; however, several were willing to take a risk and implement the blog (Principle 4). At the end of the term,

---

[21] For a simple summary, see http://www.tnellen.com/ted/tc/schein.html

success was uncertain and pressing forward for another term seems questionable (Principle 5). Schein's conceptual model of culture change illuminated the weakness of my proposed cognitive restructuring. It is now apparent that the disconfirming data did not result in enough 'survival anxiety' to reduce the 'learning anxiety' of student teachers, mentor teachers, or my colleagues. They simply did not feel a need to change, and were content to accept that the classroom attempts to merge theory and practice would continue to generate frustration, albeit minor in their estimation.

Project II. Leading as a Learning Coach (Bobbi Compton is currently a learning coach with Fort McMurray Local No 48)
My project was titled *Leading as a Learning Coach*. I proposed to further my role as a learning coach to impact staff development and student learning. I intended to show how coaching, as a part of distributed leadership, can lead to school improvement. I planned to work with staff to use *First Steps in Reading* as a tool to implement literacy changes, and I believed student learning would be positively impacted by supporting the teaching process. I believed on-site professional development and teacher collaboration would engender teaching and learning practices that engaged students and improved literacy skills. My leadership project hoped to establish coaching into the school culture; further develop my capacity as a leader; facilitate professional development; and collaborate with staff to improve literacy practice.

In September 2010, I presented my project to the school's administration team with a proposed yearlong plan to use my learning coach position to impact student development and learning including the following:

- Work with the AISI Lead and Professional Development Facilitator
- Educate staff on *First Steps in Reading*, running records, and guided reading
- Observe classroom practice, student engagement, and provide feedback
- Work with staff on different data collection methods of and for student learning
- Model teaching and collaborating with teachers
- Work with teachers on instructional approaches to *First Steps in Reading*
- Collect data to report to administrators and district leaders
- Liaise with other learning coaches, administrators, and parents

The importance of leaders and teachers working together to ensure that teaching practice meets the needs of learners is profound. While this leadership project was meant to improve learning, my focus was working with teachers on their pedagogical practice. Throughout the school year, we maintained the project focus through relationship building, ongoing collaboration, staff training in *First Steps in Reading*, monthly literacy newsletters, and classroom observations and feedback.

Although students benefited though engaged classroom teaching and learning, I am concerned that the work of learning coaching must continue to engrain site-based professional development, collaboration, classroom observations, and feedback into school culture. Recent government cutbacks might halt the continuation of leadership initiatives such as coaching in schools. My role as a learning coach emerged from AISI funding and my district's initiative and vision to support professional development. Sadly, AISI budget cutbacks during the fourth round of funding scaled back the coaching model and reduced the impact on teacher practice, student learning, future leadership opportunities, and research.

My leadership project was an opportunity to conduct action research as school improvement through leadership. The success of my leadership project was indicated by positive feedback on staff surveys, sustainability from relationships, and my administration's acknowledgement of my leadership skills. Administrative support has been crucial to my leadership project and coaching role. My district showed confidence in the learning coach model by continuing funding despite government cutbacks. I believe the project established the role of learning coach and promoted my leadership capacity. I learned the importance of building relationships and establishing strong foundations. The 2011-2012 school year was the third for the learning coach initiative and I plan to continue my leadership project and research.

Project III. Improving Parental Engagement (Melissa Humby, Buck Mountain Central School, Buck Lake, Alberta)

My project was based on parental involvement at the high school level. I targeted all parents of the students I taught, including parents who had not had involvement at school in the past; specifically at parent teacher interviews, parent council, or volunteering. I wanted parents to be more involved in their children's education, and know what was happening at school. I made positive phone calls or emails home - at least one phone call or email per student each month. I kept a log of my home communication progress.

My project goal was to encourage more parents to become part of the school community and their children's learning. One main challenge was a historical lack of parental involvement. Currently, only two or three parents attend parent council meetings. At most, twenty-five parents attend two-day parent teacher interviews. Few parents volunteer at school dances, hot lunches, school trips, or other functions. Generally, the same five or six parents volunteer for every school activity. Often parents are intimidated, view the school negatively, or are overwhelmed with their own work, family, or other activities. My school is located in a small town in rural Alberta, and often both parents work full time. Our population includes First Nations, Métis and Inuit (FNMI) students, foster parents, and single parent families – all circumstances that challenge and become obstacles to parental involvement.

In addition to several socioeconomic factors on our past

accountability pillars; teacher caring has been ranked poorly in the eyes of both parents and students. Issues identified include teachers providing few opportunities for talking with parents (whether by email or phone updates) about student progress, and updating our school website. Moreover, teachers often believe they have little time to contact every parent because we assume roles as teachers, coaches, counselors, or leaders of extra-curricular activities.

The real driver to pursue my leadership project was when a parent visited me at school. I had been the only teacher to ever call home and update her on her child's progress. I thought, "How can this be happening?" The parent had never attended parent teacher interviews, parent council meetings, or would ever consider volunteering. Essentially, the only contact she had with the school was my occasional phone calls.

I anticipated more parents would become involved in the school community and in their children's learning. My goal was to encourage teachers to make home contacts without always reporting negatives, and I aspired to see a change at the student level. If parents knew more about what was happening at school and had positive relationships and open communication with teachers, I believed this openness would help students view school in a more positive and productive manner.

At the beginning of the school year, I sent home a letter with every student I taught requesting an email address and the phone number they preferred. Several times a month, I sent personalized positive emails/phone calls to parents about their children's progress and behavior in my class. Additionally, I emailed about tests, quizzes, assignments, extra help, up-coming school events, and kept parents informed through our school website with daily school activities and homework updates. During the semester, I distributed a survey asking parents and students about their thoughts on positive parental communication. I received positive feedback from parents and students and saw encouraging progress in student behavior, class work, and homework completion. The majority of parents welcomed my emails and felt they knew more about what was happening at school. Some parents preferred phone calls. Surprisingly, students reported that they looked forward to my emailing their parents and were curious about what I said. In addition to positive feedback from parents and students, I experienced a breakdown in barriers and increased parental trust.

As a result of my project, parents become more involved at school and with their children's learning. Positive phone calls or emails helped teachers show parents they cared, and parents seemed more comfortable making contact and coming to school. Student behavior and homework completion improved. From the feedback and results, I hope to extend this project further by encouraging other staff members and teachers to do the same. Positive communication with home encourages parents whose view of the school is not positive or who might be intimidated or need a voice. At the high school level, I have found that most parental communication from teachers is negative. If they are being contacted, likely their children have done something wrong, which has warranted a phone call from school. Attempting to build positive communication is a good way to encourage parents to become more involved and have a voice.

Project IV. Informed Transformation: Improving Success for First Nations, Métis, and Inuit (FNMI) Students (Raime Drake, Eleanor Hall School, Clyde, Alberta)

During the 2010 summer course, I read Hargreaves and Shirley's (2009) *The Fourth Way – The Inspiring Future for Educational Change* and connected their ideas to improving the success of First Nations, Métis, and Inuit (FNMI) students in our schools. Although I do not hold a formal leadership position in my school, I consider myself a teacher leader with a passion for improving education for at-risk students. We have a high percentage of FNMI students at our school. At a school planning day, staff identified a need to support our FNMI students by increasing cultural awareness. Métis dancers performed at our school, and we have utilized the district FNMI liaison worker to make presentations to students. However, after reading many articles centered on social justice, I felt compelled to do more. As a teacher leader, I felt responsible to do more than 'come down from the manor', participate in an activity, then 'return to the manor' to resume my life.

Many of our staff members have no experience teaching FNMI students. I wanted staff to consider their own learning and teaching experiences to better respond to our students' needs. With full support of my principal, I led a series of discussions to raise the achievement of our FNMI students. I invited an Elder and his wife (also an educator) – Roy and Judy Louis from the Samson Cree Nation – to visit in September and speak to our entire staff. Roy enlightened our staff about traditions, protocol, spirituality, and the Cree language. He led staff through a smudge ceremony before lunch. In the afternoon, Judy spoke about learning styles and fostering relationships with students and their families. Resources were presented and discussed. We ended the day with a sharing circle where each staff member shared what he or she had learned.

I surveyed staff to find out if the information helped change their teaching practices. There was an overwhelming desire from teachers and program assistants to apply what they had learned to their classroom practice. Staff also wanted to find out where they could get more information and resources. The discussions on our PD day and results from the survey sparked conversations that have since shaped our staff meetings and professional development sessions.

I hoped this project would impact learning by acknowledging student differences as well as their similarities. By being aware of how students learn and interact with others, teachers can better create positive learning environments. As I have visited my colleagues' classrooms, I have seen many strategies being used to support FNMI students. We learned to increase the use of visual supports, place the desks in a circle, use peer teaching, and help students see the 'big picture' of assignments, and then break them into steps.

This project has also worked well with our district AISI initiative to use formative classroom assessment. Richards, Brown & Forde (2007) acknowledged, "Tests that are not sensitive to students' cultural and linguistic background will often merely indicate what the students don't know…and very little about what they do. Thus, the opportunity to build on what students know is lost" (p. 67). Teachers in my school are using alternative assessments to determine what the students know, rather than focusing strictly on summative tests and activities.

Our district FNMI liaison worker has a strong presence in our school. She also attended the PD day with our staff, and I see more staff utilizing her expertise as a result of the shared experience. She is able to facilitate connections between families and the school to support our FNMI students. As a result of this project, I commissioned an artist to sketch our school with the four traditional Métis colors held by an eagle's feather. "Our hearts and spirits for our children" is written in Cree syllabics. I presented the picture to our staff in April to celebrate the changes that have occurred in our school. The picture hangs in our foyer to remind us all of our commitment to our most at-risk learners.

The title of my project was "Informed Transformation". I believe our staff has come a long way in supporting our FNMI students. There had to be an open readiness for change. Staff recognized that following the status quo was not the answer. To bring about change, we had to re-engineer roles and responsibilities. As teachers, we must be aware of our own cultures and biases and how these affect our teaching. By understanding where our students come from, we can better address their needs rather than applying a one-size fits all approach to teaching and learning. Teachers have the responsibility to teach all students. Finally, we must be resilient. Beliefs and actions cannot be changed in one-day professional development sessions or even over the course of one year. Discussions and critical dialogue will need to continue over a long period of time to promote self-reflection and meaningful change.

Future prospects for rethinking school leadership in Alberta schools

We know that school leadership makes a difference in student learning. For example, in a large, mixed-methods study, Sammons, Gu, Day, & Ko (2011) explored the impact of school leadership (particularly the principal/head teacher) on school improvement in England. Their findings support both formal and informal links between school leadership, school improvements, and school academic performance. In other words; leadership impacts both school improvement and academic performance of students.

However, studying the impact of teacher and principal leadership is complex. Hallinger & Heck (2011) believe studies of school leadership and student learning are so influenced by school context and environment that traditional school leadership studies provide incomplete pictures of how school leadership impacts student learning. They theorize that leadership is a reciprocal, mutual-influence process, and that anyone who wishes to study this area must engage complex conceptual and methodological issues before they can understand how school leadership contributes to student learning.

So much depends upon how principals practice their work. For example, May & Supovitz (2011) examined what they called "the scope of principal efforts" (the extent to which principals target or distribute teacher instructional leadership). Obviously, principals shape instructional leadership activities differently. Some principals target the entire faculty; some focus on single teachers. May and Supovitz found that the frequency of principal instructional leadership with individual teachers directly impacts instructional changes reported by that teacher. They also found that principals who focus on instructional improvement, both with specific teachers and using broader approaches, help engage teachers in instructional leadership.

Finally, research suggests that sharing school leadership shapes teaching careers. Taylor, Yates, Meyer, & Kinsella's (2011) evaluation study found that teachers who engaged professional leadership opportunities warded off 'flat' career trajectories because they grew in subject expertise and leadership capacity as they engaged in leadership opportunities. Their findings suggest that expanded leadership roles helped experienced teachers both advance their teacher knowledge and promote educational reform.

Clearly, teacher-leaders in our course work engaged in both school improvement and instructional leadership. What have we learned from our work with teacher leaders? How might we build teacher professional learning that better supports teacher leadership? The genesis of the course emerged from working closely with the Alberta Initiative for School Improvement (AISI) and with Alberta teachers who had grown in their leadership skills and willingness to engage leadership more broadly. AISI is now entering Cycle 5 and has grown more confident in its programmed research focus. In other words, what began in 1999 as singular site-based-only school improvement projects has grown in 2012 into a site-based research agenda widely-shared and synthesized throughout the province. At each step, however, new learning has naturally pushed teacher comfort zones. It should be no surprise that fully embracing a research agenda as the focus of AISI projects demands that teachers and school division leadership take a deep breath before they plunge ahead.

As AISI enters Cycle 5, it is clear that the emergence of teacher leaders within Alberta has been a strength of AISI. What do the findings of this course suggest for future action? First, the school improvement projects in which these teachers engaged during this course suggest how invested teachers are and can be in their students' learning. Findings also suggest that teachers can read the needs of the sites where they work. Leadership projects were engaged logically, followed successfully, and altered as needed to shape the work – the very skills needed for conducting site-based research within the schools. The success of these projects suggests that teachers are able to become research leaders within their settings. As AISI Cycle 5 is engaged, this learning is key.

The success of these teacher-leaders also suggests that engaging teachers in graduate-level course work can bridge from learning to positive school actions. For example, our earlier meta-analysis of student engagement (Taylor & Parsons, 2011) found that project-based teaching promoted student engagement and learning: there is every reason to believe project-based learning would also work with teachers.

Finally, the success of these teacher-leaders offers district leaders a glimpse of how they might more fully engage teachers in creating environments and structures that support the development of teacher leaders. Research just completed on instructional leadership (Parsons & Beauchamp, 2011) found that distributed leadership was a key factor in highly-successful elementary schools. Such research suggests that engaging teachers in research leadership at the school and district site would pay huge benefits for school improvement and student learning.

In summary, the success of teachers in this single summer course shows how learning in graduate course work in education might bridge to school contexts. Such bridging offers us a picture of how Alberta teacher leadership might be specifically developed within the Alberta context, and suggests possible changes in three domains of activity:

1. How education graduate courses and programs that claim to develop teacher leaders might be improved.
2. How school division leaders might better engage and support teacher leadership within their own district.
3. How provincial level educational ministry policy people might envision how they utilize teachers as grassroots leaders in the formation of practical educational policy and activity.

References

First Steps Reading Map of Development, Canadian Edition (2008). Pearson Education Canada, Toronto ON (Copyright is named as Minister for Education and Training, Western Australia 2004).

First Steps Reading Resource Book, Canadian Edition (2008). Pearson Education Canada, Toronto ON (Copyright is named as Minister for Education and Training, Western Australia 2004).

First Steps Linking Assessment, Teaching and Learning (2008). Pearson Education Canada, Toronto ON (Copyright is named as Minister for Education and Training, Western Australia 2003)

Hallinger, P. & Heck, R. H. (2011). Conceptual and Methodological Issues in Studying School Leadership Effects as a Reciprocal Process. *School Effectiveness and School Improvement, 22*(2), 149-173.

Hargreaves, A. and Shirley, D. (2009) *The Fourth Way – The Inspiring Future for Educational Change*. Thousand Oaks, CA: Corwin (Sage).

May, H. & Supovitz, J. A. (2011). The Scope of Principal Efforts to Improve Instruction, *Educational Administration Quarterly, 47*(2), 332-352.

Parsons, J, & Beauchamp, L (2011). *Living Leadership for Learning: Case Studies of Five Alberta Elementary School Principals*. Edmonton, Canada: ATA.

Richards, H., Brown, A., Forde, T. (2007). Addressing diversity in schools: Culturally responsive pedagogy. ***Teaching Exceptional Children, 23*** (3), 64-68.

Sammons, P.; Gu, Q.; Day, C.; Ko, J. (2011). Exploring the Impact of School Leadership on Pupil Outcomes: Results from a Study of Academically Improved and Effective Schools in England. *International Journal of Educational Management, 25*(1), 83-101.

Schein, E. (2010). *Organizational culture and leadership*. (4th ed). San Francisco, CA: Jossey Bass.

Taylor, L. & Parsons, J. (2011). Improving Student Engagement. *Current Issues in Education,* 14(1). Retrieved from http://cie.asu.edu/

Taylor, M.; Yates, A.; Meyer, L. H.; & Kinsella, P. (2011). Teacher Professional Leadership in Support of Teacher Professional

Development. *Teaching and Teacher Education: An International Journal of Research and Studies, 27(1),* 85-94.

Inside-Out Leadership in Two Schools: Owning our practice as leaders in learning

Shirley J. Stiles and P. Jean Stiles[22]

When we discuss leadership in practice in schools, we usually focus on the leadership skills of the principal and the administrative staff. There is a vast literature on this topic, and there are excellent books that describe the qualities needed in a principal to lead and guide a school to educational greatness, ranging from an international perspective to an Alberta one (L. Seashore, K. Leithwood, K.L. Wahlstrom, and S.E. Anderson, 2010; J. Parsons and L. Beauchamp, 2011).

In this chapter, we present two simple but evocative examples to illustrate how leadership in schools can be extended to promote student learning and to insure that the practices become embedded in the culture of the school. This way, in the event that the principal or key teacher-leaders leave, the established practices remain central to the way learning occurs.

Schools that create and sustain the delivery of effective education for each student while actively engaging their communities have always existed. When researchers study these schools and analyze their results, they generally find that the key to their success is the truism that it is the teacher that matters (Hargreaves, 2007; Glickman, 1993; Leithwood, K., and D. Duke. 1999). Importantly, these are teachers whose leaders (the

---

[22] *The authors express their appreciation to Cora Ostermeier, principal of the Holy Family School in Grimshaw, Alberta.*

principal and other school administrators) have developed processes to create a culture where teachers take ownership of their teaching practice each and every day.

Taking ownership of professional practice to improve student learning is a powerful example of 'inside out' leadership: where teachers collaborate, celebrate, share, debate, and never stop trying new learning strategies. They believe that all students, given the right support, can learn and continue to improve their skills. With 'inside out' leadership, teachers are encouraged to make learning decisions for their students. This is "inside out" leadership at its best. For too long, school reform has been presented in the literature as a complicated and almost impossible task when, in fact, we know far more than we choose to act upon[23]. This paradox does not need to be so commonplace in our schools. 'Inside out' leadership is where the expectations for both teachers and students are clear and are set at a high level. Students know what is expected of them and also what they can expect from the teacher. Once teachers are in agreement about the expectations (not always an easy task), a clear and consistent foundation is established. Now, teachers and students

---

[23] Ben Levin, one of Canada's pre-eminent education policy analysts drives this point home in his review of government policies related to equity. See "Achieving Equity Through Innovation: A Canada-U.S. Dialogue" available at http://www.cea-ace.ca/education-canada/article/achieving-equity-through-innovation-canada-us-dialogue *Education Canada* Current Issue Winter 2012 Volume 52 Issue 1 http://www.cea-ace.ca/education-canada/article/achieving-equity-through-innovation-canada-us-dialogue. Ben Levin's new book on improving high schools will be published early in 2012 by Corwin, and Breaking Barriers, a book on equity in education co-authored with Avis Glaze and Ruth Mattingley, has just been published by Pearson.

can monitor their progress toward achievement of these expectations.

In schools with this innovative type of leadership, each teacher is considered a "teacher leader". If the principal and assistant principals are intent on this, the development of all teachers is an inherent part of all activities in and out of the classroom. In such an environment, teachers are treated as highly qualified professionals who have exciting but difficult and challenging tasks to perform each day. They must plan, create and implement learning opportunities for each student in each class that they teach. This is a seemingly insurmountable task that teachers face each day considering the number of students in their classes with their diverse backgrounds and skills. However, teachers in these schools insist that it can be achieved with the support of their fellow teachers and a strong instructional leader as the principal.

What takes place in these innovative schools is well planned and deliberate. Principals and the leadership team must have a clear, shared vision of what they believe. Each member of the leadership team must be able to articulate the vision and how it represents the best learning practices for the students in their particular community. The environment in these schools encourages teachers to reflect on their practices, to consider new ideas, and determine what would be most effective for their students. In these schools, creative procedures are developed to ensure that teachers have a variety of ways to collaborate, to create and to celebrate.

Teachers in 'inside out' schools talk about "our school, our students and our staff". It is the collective responsibility that makes these schools unique. Not all teachers will find this a comfortable work environment, but the school should not change course. When you walk into these schools, there is a feeling of excitement and vibrancy, which is almost palpable.

These schools can exist anywhere from a large urban high school to a small rural school. The requirements are the same. The communities may be very different but the results achieved can be identical. To illustrate this, we chose two vastly different schools in Alberta where we believe that 'inside out' leadership is working.

A Small but Thriving Learning Community - Holy Family School

In northern Alberta, Canada, in the small town of Grimshaw, there is a small Catholic school that serves about 200 students from kindergarten to grade 9. The community is small and somewhat remote. The school has been in existence for 50 years, and it is part of the Holy Family School District based in Peace River. The school has a diverse student population with, 31% coded as being 'special needs', 25% as FNMI (First Nations, Métis, Inuit) and a number of ELL (English Language Learners).

The principal of the school is in her third year. When interviewed, she told us that her school district is striving to help students improve in innovative and creative ways. The faculty is comprised of 16 educators and 15 support staff. The staff is hardworking, highly committed to the students, and welcoming of new ideas that are intended to enhance student learning.

To develop teacher leaders at every level in the school, the principal developed an Instructional Leadership Team consisting of six teachers who represent the three divisions of the school: kindergarten to grade 3; grades 4 to 6; and grades 7 to 9. This team, along with the principal, guides the instructional decisions for the school. They study multiple sources of data to determine the learning gaps for students. For example, many of the students are 'hands-on' learners, and the staff has been exploring ways to use assessment and differentiated instructional practices to improve learning.

The team also decides on professional development for the staff, and they are prepared to be teachers in demonstration or "model" classrooms. Team membership is typically for one year. The team meets regularly and attends professional development sessions to assist them in developing new educational and teaching skills. One of their tasks is to act as the chief communicators within the division they represent. The staff, as a whole, works to identify barriers to student learning. They clearly identify areas of need, then focus on resolving these needs. These decisions are shared regularly with parents on the school council.

Holy Family has a group of six junior high school teachers who are fairly new to the teaching profession. The principal saw the possibility of developing them into a cross-curricular team. She applied for professional development funds, and hired a consultant from the Alberta Assessment Consortium. The results show real promise.

These six teachers have received comprehensive professional development, which has helped them build and develop their expertise in the areas of assessment, planning, performance task creation, and specifically, project-based learning. This experience has enhanced the school's capacity for leadership, mentorship, engagement, and hands-on learning. The principal told us that this group of teachers has a wide range of skills, capabilities, and academic focuses. Their wide range of interests has allowed many opportunities for them to be involved in multi-tiered ways. It is an ideal group of teachers that has become ambassadors for project-based learning for the school and for the school division.

One of the practices that the principal has established is regular "learning" visits to classrooms. She does this alone, and forewarns the teachers prior to each two week period she spends visiting their classrooms. Her visits include talking to students about what they are learning, and observing a teaching skill so that she can provide feedback to the teacher. After a classroom visit, she leaves a note for the teacher about what she observed.

Teams of teachers also conduct learning visits with a focus established by the Instructional Leadership Team. Teachers being visited are given notice of these visits as well, and one of the key features is short discussions with students. It is apparent that the students are comfortable talking about their learning, and that they like hands-on learning. A positive student attitude to learning, achievement and taking ownership of their learning is observable. The principal believes that this is one of the ways student leadership will develop in the school.

The success with hands-on projects, particularly in science, has resulted in students requesting these types of projects in other subjects. The projects are displayed in the school, creating parental and community interest. Parents and members of the community have volunteered their services to work with students in their areas of expertise. For example, a co-ed Fabrics and Fashion class has been created that is led by a community member. The class has been actively engaged in making pajamas for their families. The teachers see enormous potential in having cross-curricular projects that could include mathematics, language arts and social studies.

These projects are finely tuned with assessment and performance in mind. The main objective is to expose students to project-based learning that enhances collaboration, communication, and understanding at an authentic learning level. The principal has to be creative with scheduling and finding time for the teachers to meet, to build and create their learning modules. From observing this team of teachers in action at one of their workshops, it was evident that any school would benefit from a team of teachers working together in this way.

Another effective leadership practice at Holy Family School is that the principal prepares a monthly synopsis that highlights every aspect of the school. She shares portions of this with parents, all of it with her staff, her supervisor and the superintendent of schools. Besides being a celebration, it ensures no surprises. If the principal does not have the needed resources, she finds ways to bring them into the school from outside, thereby creating more learning opportunities for the students.

For example, the students love art, but no one on staff was trained to teach it. The principal prepared a grant proposal, and she was able to hire seven artists–in-residence. They are developing student artist leaders. The principal and staff at Holy Family view every obstacle to learning as an exciting challenge to solve together.

The school understands that this is a process, and that they are on a journey that they are determined to complete with their community.

Distributed Leadership at Jasper Place High School

At the other end of the spectrum is Jasper Place (JP) High School, Edmonton, Alberta. JP is a large urban high school with 2,300 students and 160 staff, and is the largest school in the Edmonton Public School District. The school offers a broad spectrum of programs that includes International Baccalaureate, Advanced Placement, all vocational-CTS programs, and programming for a wide variety of special needs students. JP is student-centered, and has a vision that guarantees success for each student that enters the school. While this might sound like a 'pie in the sky' or a 'motherhood' dream, it is evident when walking through the school and talking to students, staff, and parents that pathways to success are found for all students. The school has developed leadership on three levels: student leadership, whole schoolteacher leadership, and the formal instructional leadership team.

To make the school truly student-centered and responsive to student needs, it was imperative for the school administration to know what students felt about their learning environment and learning experiences. They developed and honored an authentic 'student voice'. This was achieved by meeting with students in a variety of forums and asking questions, including some difficult and sensitive questions about the school environment. To gain student trust, they made sure that students could see that their opinions were being heard, and that actions emerged from their input and feedback. Principal advisory groups were established, featuring diverse groups of students that met on a regular basis with the principal and the school's administrative team; for example, meetings with the Leading Spirits Aboriginal Group.

Another productive way the school assessed the learning environment was by classroom visits and internal 'walk-throughs' with specific objectives for observing the teaching and learning. The walk-throughs were conducted by separate groups of teachers, students and parents. This provided a great insight to the learning environment, and the comfort that the students felt with their learning goals. The teachers and students were comfortable with visitors in their classrooms. Students articulated what they were learning, why they were learning it, and how they accessed assistance if the learning was not going as well as expected. This year, the school opened a Global Café to showcase student talent, and to teach students how to question the *status quo*, how to become involved citizens, and how to interact more frequently with community partners. Although this is in the beginning stages, the students involved with the Global Café are already emerging as a strong 'student voice'.

Each teacher on staff has a role of being a teacher leader at JP. They meet weekly to share professional development, discuss classroom practice, share ideas about students, and collaborate. Teachers make sure no students fall 'through the cracks' without an intervention. They know that their relationships with students create a positive school climate, and are what makes the difference to students' success.

Teachers each 'adopt' an 'at risk' student in their class to help get him or her 'across the line'. In many cases, teachers have 'adopted' more than one student. They know that there is adequate support in the school for students who are severely at risk, so the administration asked that the adopted students not be the most severe cases, but rather those students that will really benefit from the extra TLC. The adopted student could be an individual who is simply at risk of not reaching their potential. Teachers are given the opportunity to share 'at risk' strategies that have or have not worked. This creates an environment of trust where successes and failures are shared. Each teacher also acts as an IPP (Individual Program Plan) coordinator for at least one of the special needs, coded students. The teacher may or may not teach that student; teachers hold a draft each year to secure their position in working with their student. In many cases, a teacher will have a student over a three year period.

This range of strategies has developed a school climate where the staff talks about students as "our" students. Students and parents talk about feeling that the school cares for all students, and the school staff know that they make a difference in students' learning lives at JP.

Teacher leaders that hold formal leadership positions (at JP - the Faculty Council) are approximately 25 percent of the teaching staff. These department heads, curriculum coordinators and assistant principals are key to creating an environment in which students are always at the center, and teachers feel valued and respected. Teachers are supported to enhance their instructional (classroom) practices, and there is a culture of innovation and risk-taking. Members of Faculty Council are expected to model these qualities, and they are charged with assisting teachers in their departments to achieve these goals. This does not happen because the members of the Faculty Council are the most senior or have the best content knowledge. It happens because teachers are trained to take on the role of instructional leader. This happens because there has been intentional training and modeling for the Faculty Council.

The principal and administration team provide on-going professional development for the Faculty Council. Each member of this leadership team has a coach and is coached by another member of the team. *These teacher leaders are living in a data-rich environment with qualitative and quantitative information as well as internal and external measures.* The data are used to ask questions about teaching practices, and to question whether the actions are in the best interests of the students. Each member of the leadership team is responsible for his or her department, but the leadership team also meets regularly in cross-curricular groups. Each member of the leadership team is responsible for hosting discussions with three or four other members of staff on a regular basis. Limiting the size of the groups allows all voices to be heard.

Leading From the Inside Out

While school improvement research represents a vast body of thinking, we see it cohering around five main factors that impact student learning:

- i) a society's views toward students and education;
- ii) curriculum - what we teach;
- iii) the quality of teachers;
- iv) school climate; and
- v) the impacts of peers.

While many think that it is the students' peers that are the greatest influence, in 'inside out' schools, it is unquestionably their teachers. Teachers represent society to the students. Our work reminds us continually that, aside from their parents, teachers are the most visible daily evidence of society's commitment to students. Teachers are the facilitators of the curriculum, and they bring it to life for the students.

School climate is difficult to quantify, but teachers set it with their daily behavior in and out of the classroom; with their body language, voice, tone and interactions with everyone. In a school that exhibits leadership from the 'inside out', the climate set by teachers is clearly evident. Students never expect teachers to be sad, tired, bored, to go to the bathroom, to have weekends off, or ever to lose interest in them. It is one of the wonderful attitudes of youth.

In schools where teachers and their leaders genuinely believe in their students, success is evident every day. Teachers are their role models, and this reinforces why teachers choose to enter the teaching profession. Teachers have the real privilege to help shape their students' future. The challenge is to turn all teachers into teacher leaders. A quote from Haim Ginott, psychologist, educator and author of books on the relationships between children and adults (especially teachers), says it all.

> I have come to a frightening conclusion. I am the decisive element in the classroom. It is my personal approach that creates the climate. It is my daily mood that makes the weather. As a teacher I possess tremendous power to make a child's life miserable or joyous…In all situations it is my response that decides whether it will be escalated or de-escalated, and a child humanized or de-humanized (Ginott, 1965).

Stephen Murgatroyd, a widely respected observer of Alberta's education sector, has laid out six propositions that are critical for schools to be really successful:

1. Schools are the vehicles for the education of young people.
2. Learning to learn is the primary work of schools.
3. Problem-based work should be the primary focus.

4. Teachers should facilitate learning.
5. Testing should be relevant, meaningful and help students perform to their best.
6. Schools should be personal. (Murgatroyd, 2011)

Examining our case studies of two vastly different schools through the lens of the six propositions, we believe that these critical elements are present in each school. While on the surface appearing to be different, they are essentially lived out daily in fundamentally the same ways.

References

Parsons, J and L Beauchamp. 2011. *Reflecting on Leadership for Learning—Case Studies of Five Alberta Elementary School Principals.* Edmonton AB. Barnett House Press.

Ginott, H. 1965. *Teacher and child: A book for parents and teachers.* New York, NY: Collier. http://thinkexist.com/quotation/i-ve-come-to-the-frightening-conclusioin-that-i/347295.html

Glickman, Carl D.1993 Renewing America's Schools, The Jossey-Bass Education Series, Jossey-Bass, San Francisco.

Hargreaves, A. 2007. "The Long and Short of Educational Change," Education Canada, Vol. 47, no. 3, Summer.

Leithwood, K., and D. Duke. 1999. "A Century's Quest to Understand School Leadership." In Handbook of Research on Educational Administration, 2nd ed., eds. J. Murphy and K. Seashore Louis. San Francisco, Calif.: Jossey-Bass.

Murgatroyd, S. 2011. *Rethinking Education—Learning and the New Renaissance*. Edmonton: future**THINK** Press.

Seashore, Louis; K Leithwood; K L Wahlstrom; and S E Anderson. 2010. *Investigating the Links to Improved Student Learning*. University of Minnesota and University of Toronto. See executive summary http://www.cehd.umn.edu/CAREI/Leadership/Learning-from-Leadership_Executive-Summary_July-2010.pdf

Fourth Way FINAL: The Power of the Internationalization of Networks of School Leaders
Karen Lam and Dennis Shirley

Finland and Alberta demonstrate impressive rankings on the Programme for International Student Assessment (PISA) tests of the Organization for Economic Cooperation and Development (OECD). Whether on reading, writing, math, or science, the results are near or at the very top. In a global policy context in which anxious public and policy makers worry about the ability of their students to navigate the many challenges of economic growth, population mobility, and climate change, it would seem that Finland and Alberta both have much to teach others who are trying to improve their schools and their societies.

But an iron law of educational change seems to be that change almost always looks better at the macro-level of government than at the micro-level of the individual classroom in the individual school. One of us has seen this through years of intense study with the Boston Public Schools, which have been celebrated far and wide as beacons of hope in the U.S. public school system but which in terms of their prosaic everyday challenges struggle along, often with enormous injustices in terms of resourcing and teacher quality from one school to another. The other one of us has worked as a teacher leader and researcher in the context of Singapore; another widely-heralded high achieving system that places phenomenal pressure on its young people to excel on secondary school placement exams.

These lessons invite educators to take a closer look at what actually is going on in high-achieving jurisdictions. Several years ago policy makers were surprised by data (World Health Organization, 2001-2002, 2005-2006) indicating that Finnish youth were the least likely out of 34 nations to indicate that they felt good at school.[24] Alberta, on the other hand, suffers with the second highest high school dropout rate of all of Canada's provinces (Human Resources and Skills Development Canada, 2012). Although the educational problems of Alberta are a far cry from those suffered by schools in the United Kingdom or the United States, for example, it still is easy to find teachers in Alberta who feel unappreciated by the public and micro-managed by government when it comes to the freedom to develop innovative curricula. This problem persists in spite of many years of government provisioning for an innovative network like the Alberta Initiative for School Improvement (AISI), designed to promote bottom-up change and experimentation. Furthermore, Finland and Alberta are not immune from problems with substance abuse, bullying, and random shootings that perplex educators around the world.

The sordid, on-the-ground realities of life in schools as they *actually* exist in the here and now - with struggling students, querulous faculties, and anxious and sometimes pushy parents - do not mean that Finland and Alberta have not accomplished a great deal of good with their educational systems. It means,

---

[24] For further discussion and analysis on the sense of disengagement reported by Finnish students, see Linnakyla and Malin (2008). The study was conducted by the OECD as part of PISA 2003. Details are in Willms (2003).

rather, that the educational work is far from done and that each jurisdiction must resist the siren call of complacency in the light of their achievement results. Yet behind every celebration of high achievement stands the stultifying specter of apathy. So how can we improve learning, and do so in a way that all of our students will find their schools places of fulfillment and joy, and our teachers have the right combination of pressure and support to help them reach their full potential as educators?

One of the more intriguing strategies explored in a variety of jurisdictions in recent years has been to network educators together, in the belief that by exposing classroom teachers to novel practices in different settings, their internal sense of motivation and drive will be catalyzed to probe more deeply into improving their teaching and learning. In some contexts, this kind of networking has occurred within schools and in other cases across schools and even across district boundaries. In Singapore, for example, it is common to find classroom teachers who have been seconded to the Ministry of Education or to the National Institute of Education. The goal is to break down different silos within the field of education and to create a continual flow of information that links theory, policy, and practice into a vibrant and coherent profession.

Rarely, however, have educators had the opportunity to develop networks across geographically distant high-achieving jurisdictions and to inquire after the endless variety of instructional strategies, curricular designs, assessment instruments and organizational forms that make up what British sociologist Basil Bernstein (1975) called the four "message systems" of schools. It is here that Finland and Alberta are exploring the sharp edge of educational change in what is termed the Finland-Alberta or FINAL partnership.

Ignited in May 2010 at a Finnish-Canadian Education Forum in Helsinki, this alliance began with conversations about opportunities and challenges in educational change that both jurisdictions faced. The Forum's Chair, Pasi Sahlberg, spoke of the sea of opportunities possible from a new strategic partnership, while Andy Hargreaves from Boston College emphasized the importance of an evolving and sustaining international dialogue that would develop by building on the divergent strengths of the Finnish and Alberta experiences. Hargreaves cautioned against the continued reliance on approaches such as standardized curricula, technology disconnected from students' life experiences, and system-level reforms that are imposed on teachers without their consent or approval. Sahlberg provided a moving account of the Finnish experience and advanced the promise of "Fourth Way Finland" as an inspiring alternative pathway to counter the global education reform movements (GERM) that privilege system level reforms over school-based reforms (Sahlberg, 2011).

This first meeting in Spring 2010 seeded many ensuing conversations and exchanges, with follow up meetings in August in Jasper, Alberta, and in November in Boston, Massachusetts. At these events both parties identified aspirational goals and developed an action plan to attain them. This culminated in

December 2010 with letters of understanding exchanged between the Alberta Teachers' Association, the Minister of Education in Alberta, and the Finnish Ministry of Education and Culture in Helsinki. The first exciting step for this nascent partnership was for a Finnish delegation to visit selected high schools in Alberta. An invitational symposium, *Educational Futures – International Perspectives on Innovation from the Inside Out* was held in Edmonton, Alberta in March 2011. This pioneering international partnership took flight with a team of 13 Finnish high school principals and ministry officials visiting Albertan high schools in Crowsnest Pass, Calgary, Edmonton and Grande Prairie. Two months later, 19 Alberta educators made their journey towards Finland to be acquainted with approaches taken in Finnish schools.

What did educators aspire towards through this high level exchange? The FINAL partnership is transformational in that it is about the professionals themselves and their students developing school reform. Most high-level exchanges across countries are mostly confined to senior policy-makers. The FINAL network, on the other hand, reaches all the way into the domain that matters most - that of the individual, the school and classroom. FINAL is pursuing an altogether different strategy in educational change and reform that is bottom-up and side-to-side rather than top-down. As such, FINAL is a brilliant manifestation of what is described elsewhere as the "integrating networks" component of "Fourth Way" change architecture (Hargreaves & Shirley, 2009, pp. 99-101). This approach arises from a firm commitment and belief that if the professionals who work in schools everyday are provided with real cross-cultural learning opportunities, the benefits in terms of innovation, learning, and motivation will be enormous.

Stephen Murgatroyd, adviser to the FINAL network, posed the apparently simple but actually intellectual demanding question to the Albertan and Finnish delegations in spring 2011: "What makes a great school?" This question has required the educators to dig down deep to clarify their beliefs, purposes, and aspirations as educators. It has forced them to ask after their own their theories of educational change and what they mean for the students they are interacting with on a daily basis.

The following twin portraits reveal how Albertan educators In the FINAL partnership are improving the ways they support pupil learning and have implemented changes in their schools as a consequence of their participation in this project. Based on these two case studies, we distill distinctive features of teacher leadership that arise from cross-cultural learning opportunities. To this end, we provide evidence to illustrate how FINAL is providing a fresh impetus for teacher leadership that places educators in the front end rather than at the back door of change.

Jean Stiles: Modeling Continual Learning and Growth

Jean Stiles is the fast-paced, fun-loving, and zestfully enthusiastic principal at Jasper Place High School in Edmonton, Canada. An innovative and inspiring educator for 23 years, Jean has taught and been a principal at the elementary, junior, and senior high school levels. To accompany her through the halls of Jasper Place is to get caught up in a dizzying whirlwind of question and answer with her students, reaching all the way from the cliques that dominate the front entrance of the building to the almost painfully shy immigrant students who are still finding their footing in their new country.

In 2007, Jean earned the highly competitive award of "Canada's Most Outstanding Principals." She uses her passion for student learning to challenge her faculty, to share her own ongoing search for better ways to teach and lead, and to have a ball of a good time when doing it. She is completely at home in the hallways of her school and her students all know it and love it. She is also the recipient of the Learning Partnership's National Award. In recognition of her many contributions to education, Jean was inducted into Canada's National Principal Academy in 2007.

Jasper Place High School has a diverse population with programs to accommodate them that range from innovative apprenticeships to the most challenging academic courses. As a Canadian immigrant herself, Jean knows well the sense of displacement and uncertainty that new students can experience when trying to fit into a country far different from their countries of origin. This sense of compassion and her pronounced ethic of care permeate all aspects of her leadership.

Jean wants her teachers to grow as inspiring role models for their students. She knows the wide range of research documenting the distortions that can ensue when teachers become locked in professional cultures tragically organized against their own continual learning. This means that she urges teachers to grow as leaders and to share their exploration of the profession with each other and with their students.

As principal, Jean views teacher leaders as having three primary characteristics. First, teachers must model instructional excellence so that their students are enthusiastic and grow in confidence and knowledge each and every day. Second, teachers should be innovators who are willing to test out new research-based practices to expand their pedagogical repertoires. Finally, experienced teachers have a professional responsibility for working with weaker teachers. Developing such leadership is difficult because it goes against the grain of how teachers are prepared and how they work on a daily basis in schools. "How do we influence teachers from a principal perspective," she asks, "because there is such autonomy within a classroom?"

Looking at the curriculum with a new set of eyes
Curriculum is more than just *what* is taught; frequently, it also encompasses *how* teaching is carried out. In Finland, "classroom teaching is very personal," and as a result of this, educators there adopt a flexible approach to looking at the curriculum. What impressed Jean and her teachers was that Finnish teachers seemed to "have this ability to get together and build on the thematic kinds of connections within a number of curricula and put those together as a course." Inspired by this, Jean's teachers have started to look at the curriculum at Jasper Place High School with "a new set of eyes."

Jean's teachers asked themselves if the types of programs they offered were due to "the way we've set ourselves up, our structures" and wondered if in spite of their practical value, they might be "getting in the way" of deeper kinds of student learning. After much deep discussions and reflections, Jean's teachers decided that they could do better. They then examined different programs of study, found a number of connections between them that had not been made in the past, and "built on that to make different kinds of courses".

The new kinds of courses would allow for greater integration across subject lines. Building a 'school-within-a-school' also led to Jean and her teachers to challenge the usual assumptions related to class size and scheduling. They decided that they were still tied to the industrial class model, and wanted to make a change.

> What we are looking at for next year, is taking a number of kids, say 120, and giving them five teachers from different subject areas, and just having a program for them, come from an appreciative inquiry kind of place, look at those natural connections. [There is no need] to worry about 80 min. classes. But to look at what makes sense for kids and to try to build a school-within-a-school. And try to break away from some of the ways we've tried to look at the schedule, driving what we're trying to drive, driving instructional decisions.

Looking at the curriculum with new eyes also means re-evaluating the standard emphasis placed on academic learning. In fact, according to Jean, a hot topic that permeates the informal network sessions among Albertan principals is its vocational piece dimensions. And since returning from the visit to Finland,

Jean and one of her teachers have already started to shake things up.

One of the strategic approaches is to partner with the community. While in Finland, Jean and her colleagues were impressed with the "far better connections into industry, into business than what we have." Upon their return, this was an area that the Jasper Place High staff decided that they would get "really intentional about ... and really setting up those systems, and those partnerships." The change is being initiated at the teacher level, and the project was inspired by the Finns' approach to vocational education.

Finnish society views vocational education as providing students with entry into multiple paths. One of Jean's teachers, who is the school's work-experience coordinator, noted that in Finland, when a student reveals that he or she enjoys animal science, the response is not to tell the child "go and be a vet'. Instead, teachers would recommend over 50 different possible vocations to the student. In addition, the Jasper Place High School team also noticed that industry was coming to work with the schools more in Finland than they did back home in Alberta. In fact, when entrepreneurs worked with schools, they presented their latest product prototype for students to work on and to learn from. This enables students to develop the most cutting-edge and market-savvy skills and to have the opportunity to use the newest and best technology. To this end, the entrepreneurs wanted students "to have a certain level, skill-wise that will allow them to ...work for [the company]."

This experience enabled the Jasper Place High School teachers to think of their school "in a different way." On their return, they did not hesitate to accept the offer of a business association that approached the school with an idea of talking to students about starting a small business. Mindful of what they had just seen in Finland, Jasper Place educators organized a two-day session with these business mentors that was attended by 210 grade 10 students. According to Jean, this event "opened the eyes of [the students] who are starting to think about what's out there as they start to think about next steps."

Leveraging on the idea of a vocational track, Jean's teachers next developed new internship programs for their students, with the aim of "getting kids into a work place or having them experience a different side of things." The team established a new partnership with Habitat for Humanity. This out-of-school experience was novel for two reasons: it was not something carried out during the summer, and the students were not paid for the internship. The aim was for them to have a real-life experience affiliated with, but also independent from their school, as apprenticeships are organized in Finland.

Finally, in terms of new perspectives gleaned from exposure in Finland, Jean's teachers challenged the idea of single-age learning experiences. They combined this idea with community involvement in the Global Youth Assembly program. In this multi-graded approach, the teachers worked with 80 students who were interested in a film course and in an art course. The final piece for the film course was the creation of the opening film for the Global Youth Assembly.

> What students had to do to get to the final product was to research the politics of water, get involved with all the community members, and public interest groups around the politics of water. Take a whole lot of instruction from their teachers and from the community groups about film making. And the final part of the film was that they became roving reporters, activist media reporters, to put together this event for the film, the Global Youth Assembly. It's something we've never done.

At the end of the day, key features of making a "school-within-a-school" was to find ways to "make curriculum more relevant, more integrated for kids". To this end, as a leader, Jean was "always looking for ways to transform the teaching and learning for kids to make it even more relevant for them." As such, her teachers were tireless in their efforts to "think about what practical ideas [they] can put in place."

Encouraging grassroots change

Although she is the principal, Jean believes in distributing her leadership because this allows her to "see in a more open environment to help make decisions". Arising from the Finland visit, she has noticed that her teachers "have seen the things in Finland, and they are willing to try some new things". As a result, the staff at Jasper Place High School is having school-wide conversations, and teachers are going up to Jean with "far more ideas than what they might try to get there". At such sessions, Jean's teachers are "talking about projects that they want to do".

One product of these rich conversations is a social media platform that her teachers want to set up between Finland and Alberta. Since travel costs between Alberta and Finland are expensive, social media provide an easy and instant way for educators and their students to strengthen the FINAL partnership while saving on costs. The aim is for teachers from both jurisdictions to comment on student art and to learn from one another about how art is assessed in their different school contexts. In a recent article (Stiles, 2011), Jean described this project:

> ...in an art project, an Alberta teacher will share her assessment practices with her Finnish counterpart as they each assess the work of the other students and discuss the assessment process and how it affects their personal assessment strategies. Sharing teaching practices leads to informed thought about what makes a great school.

Grassroots change is most compelling when teachers remain for longer periods in each school. Unlike the situation in Canada where educators (teachers and principals alike) often change schools every four to five years, in Finland, highly-mobile teachers are viewed as undesirable and educators tend to wonder "what are you hiding from?" It is common for principals to stay in one school for the whole of their careers, thereby providing communities with a source of stability and continuity over time. This permanence is the same with teachers; the Finns view staying put "as a huge positive that people will stay and build that family." Building on this idea, Jean has a new appreciation for "the stability [that] is allowing [her] and the staff to be even more creative" than before.

Ian Baxter: Building Social Relationships to Enhance Learning

Ian Baxter is the assistant principal and a social studies teacher at Crowsnest Consolidated High School in the Livingstone Range School District of Alberta. He has been teaching social studies in the school for 19 years and prides himself on his fierce loyalty and commitment to his school of only 319 students. While some urban educators might view remote Crowsnest as too isolated, Ian loves the sense of community, the closeness to nature, and the flexibility and creativity offered in a small school environment where one can get to know all students well.

Situated in the Albertan Mountains, Crowsnest Consolidated High School serves grades 7 to 12. Ian is grateful to live in one of the most beautiful areas of Alberta. The school has been experiencing waves of out-migration. The reduction in student numbers means that the school is unable to provide as wide a variety of activities and courses as the teachers would like to offer. And for Ian, and his principal, Wes Wescott, participating in the international partnership has provided opportunities to discover new ways to embark on their mission as educators. More importantly, the partnership has also enabled them to interact with other Alberta principals.

The compelling question guiding Ian throughout his participation in the partnership is "What makes a good school?" For Ian, this is not a question simply for educators and administrators to grapple with, but it is a pertinent and significant question for the students that he interacts with daily. To this end, Ian invites his students to respond to questions such as, "How does what we do here and everyday make us a good school?" He is amazed and heartened at the responses from his students and the clarity with which they want good relationships with their teachers. "They can tell the teachers who want to work with kids, and those who are collecting a paycheck and just putting in time," Ian stated.

When Ian's students watched Finnish educators touring their school, they realized that partnerships with other schools from other parts of the world are some of the building blocks of "a good school" in today's context. Outside educators bring fresh energy, new perspectives, and a greater global awareness to their collective lives. Ian believes that in a good school, educators need to be in the thick of the action, teaching classes and interacting with students from the start to the end of each day. It is important to him, that his students see him as an educator and not merely an administrator. For this reason, Ian and Wes stand and greet every student entering their school building each day.

For Ian, involvement in the FINAL network has given him the opportunity to examine how Finnish colleagues have provided enriching and meaningful learning for their students, to meet their needs, and to ensure a purposeful life. Though the visit was short, Ian was impressed with many aspects of the Finnish education system. He had flown to Helsinki with Stephen Harris, the Assistant to the Superintendent, and when they returned from their visit they proceeded to propose some new changes for his school and its Livingston Range District. he changes they sought indicate how educators like Ian are using the FINAL network to challenge their thinking about previous patterns in their schools and to integrate in new findings about Finnish practices that they believe will benefit their students back home in Alberta.

Meeting basic needs

According to Abraham Maslow's (1954) classic hierarchy of needs, basic or "deficiency" needs at the *physiological* level, including breathing, food, water, and sleep, must be provided before moving on to high levels. For Ian, this is a "great reference to use when educating students." He wonders that if students do not have their basic needs met, "how can they possibly move up to higher level thinking?" In the close to two decades that Ian has worked as a teacher, he has noticed that increasingly more students have been showing up in school hungry and upset. And these students are not just those who come from struggling families. As an observant educator, Ian is sad that many students try to "disguise" their troubles and issues. However, when the problems persist, and students "are trying to juggle more things … it all implodes on them."

To this end, Ian and Wes were inspired by the social support provided at a Finnish school they visited – free five-course hot meals were at breakfast and lunch daily. Ian and his principal were so motivated that upon their return to Alberta, they started "an experiment to see how it works". As with all innovations, the project started off on a small-scale at Crowsnest Consolidated High School, serving breakfast twice a week to all students, not just for those "deemed in need". In fact, "any student in the school that feels that they need breakfast" is able to stop by. Ian laughs and says that their breakfast is not as luxurious as what is served in Finland - it's just "cereal and milk, or toast and jam. And [they've] been providing some yoghurt" as well.

Other than meeting students' basic needs, Ian feels that there is community building when students sit down and dine together in school. In his view, with the Finnish students they saw "having their lunch [in school], it was very much part of the school community," in contrast to Albertan students leaving campus to purchase their meals at neighbourhood stores. Ian and Wes hope that community building through dining together will be something that they can improve upon at Crowsnest High. With the provision of breakfast a success, Ian hopes to serve lunch as well. However, he adds that the school will need to seek sponsors for this. To this end, his plan is to look for a corporate sponsor at the end of 2012, if the breakfast experiment is successful.

Meeting educational needs
One learning point for Albertan leaders participating in FINAL is to broaden their definition of success. This is based on the features and structures in the Finnish education system that educators, like Ian, identified as being able to benefit Alberta students academically and vocationally. In fact, the Finnish approach to vocational education has impressed several of the

Albertan educators we spoke with. For one, Ian points out the types of skill-sets being introduced in the vocational programs in Finland were those that students "need to lead a purposeful and fulfilled life". Unlike the relentless emphasis on academic achievement in Alberta, Ian observes that teachers were "really directing and giving choice to students", especially if these students were keen to enter vocational programs. The Finnish approach was to help students develop skills "that would provide an income for them, and a lifestyle". Ian was also struck that students were not coerced into such paths but were "actually engaged" in the learning.

Examples of such programs include the welding class in which students were building fire pits, and the greenhouse project that involved students building stone walls as their final project. He commented that the students they spoke to were very positive and engaged in their work, contrary to the findings in some international studies which report that Finnish students are disengaged.

Eager to provide a similar educational path for Alberta students who are interested in vocational education, Ian and Wes approached their board administrators to engage a vocational teacher for their school to teach "small engines". Their passionate appeal to cater to the needs of disengaged students was successful when a vocational teacher was hired for their school.

One of the challenges in providing a wider range of educational programs in the Crowsnest area is the declining population and resource constraints. Yet, administrators were supportive.

Stephen Harris, assistant to the superintendent of the area remembers Ian and Wes being "incredibly strong advocates" of the trades programs which they saw in Finland. Leveraging on the partnership to "look outside the box to Finland", the board decided to support Ian and Wes' idea to provide an education that "allows more students to find their gifts."

Through the FINAL partnership, Ian also learned about new ideas to provide a wider range of curricular academic experiences for his students. In fact, Ian says that "this partnership has done a lot in terms of creating partnerships within schools…in Alberta." For instance, Ian and Wes, through discussions with colleagues from a school in Calgary, found an innovative way to re-structure the way they scheduled science lessons. Although the partnership began between Finland and Alberta, there have been many benefits within the province because the educators were "staring to find out that there're a lot of partnerships starting to emerge between teachers, and educators, and administrators." While this was not planned as one of the initial outcomes, for Ian, "it's certainly one of the outcomes that have come about."

The FINAL partnership has provided educators like Jean Stiles in Edmonton and Ian Baxter in Livingstone Range with the opportunity to better understand and change their schools, while at the same time hosting Finnish educators who likewise are reflecting upon and shifting their schools back home. Greater openness to apprenticeships, addressing students' basic needs, and enhancing a sense of community are all facets of education that Albertan educators are appreciating and adapting as a result of their novel exchange with Finland. It is becoming clear that there are many paths to the excellent learning outcomes that are measured on international assessments, and that real educators will probe beyond the surface level of tests to ask after what their students really are experiencing in school.

The Practical Wisdom of School Leadership

Based on the two portraits of Jean and Ian, what can we say about educational leadership and how it enhances and energizes learning in schools for teachers and students? Both Jean and Ian work lead schools serving different student populations in Alberta. Along with their colleagues, both journeyed to Finland and interacted with Finnish educators and students, and were inspired by aspects which they identified could make a difference to "what makes a great school" for their students. Upon their return, both enthusiastically and energetically entered into conversation with colleagues, administrators, and students, and in both cases, initiated structural and cultural changes to their school, and district.

Far too often, change is top-down and *done* to teachers and schools, without careful consideration of local needs and contexts. As a result, there is a misalignment between the policy intent and the realities and practices in the classroom and school. In this study, we found evidence of *bottom-up* and *side-to-side* school and curricula change; bottom-up change emanates from the schools and educators themselves in response to challenging current assumptions and structures while in side-to-side change, educators took the onus on themselves to catalyze and cascade within and across their own contexts and localities. Specifically, with reference to *side-to-side* change, both Jean and Ian actively organized sessions in which they presented their experiences in Finland to colleagues. Additionally, Ian built on conversations with colleagues in Calgary to review the science curriculum in his school. In Edmonton, Jean and her teachers created a model of *side-to-side* change when teachers responsible for different grade levels collaborated to develop a multi-grade learning experience.

Building on Jean and Ian's experiences and also through interviews and conversations with other Albertan educators participating in this partnership, we identified and distilled three distinctive features of FINAL as a Fourth Way change strategy. First, FINAL is guided by an inspiring, innovative, and inclusive vision. Second, it involves lively learning communities that welcome contestation and debate rather than "contrived collegiality" (Hargreaves, 1994, p. 186) that meets someone else's predetermined goals. Third, FINAL is an integrating network with the right calibration of emergence and design to allow for both creative and practical, measurable outcomes.

Inspiring, innovative and inclusive vision
The educators presented in our case studies are driven by a compelling and inclusive moral purpose that serves as the beacon guiding their work. Their vision of educational outcomes transcends narrow academic achievement and acknowledges the cultural richness and complexity of the whole child. For

educators such as Jean and Ian, graduating students do not resemble cookies created by a cookie-cutter mold or a faceless product with a manufacture date.

How is this humanistic philosophy of education communicated to students? One way is through a school's web site. At Jasper Place High School in Edmonton, (http://jasperplace.epsb.ca/rebels-define) each student entering the gates of Jasper High School is seen as "a rebel" – an individual "who stands out from the crowd," "an inquisitive person who embraces a challenge," and a "passionate, adventurous, and fearless character." Another way is through active listening to student voice. At Crowsnest High, student voice is valued, appreciated, and incorporated in all of its internal discussions exploring the question: "What is a good school?" The staff at Crowsnest is mindful that meeting students' physiological, psychological, and emotional needs is as significant as developing them intellectually and socially.

Jean, Ian and their colleagues strive to meet each child's different needs and interests. This is why this group of educators was deeply moved and inspired by the Finnish approach to vocational education, strong and efficient social support, and curriculum programs. Motivated and guided by the ideas gleaned from their trip to Finland in May 2011, these educators and their colleagues wasted no time upon their return to Alberta in challenging traditional assumptions regarding vocational education. While tweaking the traditional message systems of teaching and schooling, these educators have not disregarded the emphasis on literacy and numeracy that society deems as critical for entry to college programs. What steers these educators is their deep commitment to meeting the interests of students who are disinclined and disinterested in academic college programs, but are keen on practical, applied learning.

The vision of the FINAL network provides a striking point of contrast to the Global Educational Reform Movement (GERM) described by Finnish educator and FINAL co-founder Pasi Sahlberg (2011). Promoted by transnational consultancies linked with a corporate reform agenda, these consultancies recommend continual standardization blended with marketplace models of change as the strategies of choice for those who would seek to improve teaching and learning. But there are other ways of conceptualizing change. One of us has worked in Singapore where "white space" has been created in the curriculum for teachers to create school-based curriculum innovations. This movement is part of a call from Singapore's Prime Minister for teachers to "teach less" so that students can "learn more" (Lee, 2004). This compelling vision conceives education as preparing students for the "test of life" rather than a "life of tests" (Shanmugartnam, 2005). Like the "white space reform" in Singapore, the FINAL partnership between Finland and Alberta provides educators with another way of understanding their work, and policymakers with another set of options to consider.

Lively learning communities
In his classic investigation, *Schoolteacher: A Sociological Study* (1975, p. 14), Dan Lortie wrote about the "egg crate school", in

which teachers work individually and in isolation within their classrooms. This cellular nature of teaching does not provide teachers with opportunities to interact and learn from each other. What we have seen from the FINAL partnership is that, when provided the opportunity, educators are enthusiastic and eager to exchange ideas with colleagues in the partnership, and then with colleagues back in their respective jurisdictions. Both Jean and Ian tell compelling narratives of their conversations with the teachers in their schools, as well as with other Albertan educators. As Jean remarked, such communities are sustained by the retention of staff, who by the length of their tenure in a school, contribute towards the building of "family" in the school.

These lively learning communities are not confined to teachers but extended to students. Ian speaks of how he engages his students to discuss the features of a good school, and Jean describes the interactions between her students and their Finnish peers. These learning communities are enhanced when the school leadership is open and receptive to teacher ideas, and there platforms for school-wide and also district- and province-wide conversations. Through these conversations, creative ideas are gleaned, and best practices are shared. Ian's vignette of how a conversation with Calgary educators led his school to review their Science curriculum is particularly significant because of the genuine desire to learn about the creative approaches in other schools. Likewise, Jean's example of the transnational online assessment project illustrates that physical distance does not deter or obstruct educators who are eager to learn from each other.

A significant observation is that these communities are driven by the purpose, need and vision of the local context, rather than by externally imposed goals and targets. At Jean's school, the creation of the Global Youth Assembly was based on a group of teachers seeking to create a richer learning experience through multi-age learning. At Ian's school, the faculty's decision to provide breakfast was more than meeting students' physical needs; it was also a way for teachers and students to deepen their interaction with and engagement with the school community. These kinds of school communities, driven by moral purpose and anchored in high levels of communication and exchange around that purpose, are more likely to be sustainable in the long term (Fullan, 2004; Hargreaves & Fink, 2005).

Integrating networks of school leaders across international boundaries

The educators participating in the Finnish-Albertan partnership have gleaned deep insights about educational structures, teaching cultures, and curriculum offerings as they visited each other's jurisdictions. These site visits have provided rich learning for the teachers because they learned by experience, and by watching their colleagues in action. For such conversations and learning to deepen, it is crucial that the learning continues back in their own jurisdictions. These teachers were active in sharing their experiences with their colleagues in school, as well as those in other schools. In addition to the international partnership, the Albertan teachers developed and intensified conversations at different scales: communication among principals, teachers, and students across and within districts and jurisdictions. To this end, subsidiary and complementary nodes of communication have evolved from this international partnership. The emerging network is multi-level, integrated, and nested. This is one feature of integrated networks, where deep learning cascades beyond the handful of participating teachers to reach colleagues within and across the two jurisdictions.

Ian and Wes connected with principals in their local area, and Jean's teachers collaborated in a virtual learning community with their Finnish counterparts to discuss assessment matters. Through these informal and formal networks, the teachers had access to a variety of expertise, such as drawing externally from the local business community, and internally within their own school communities. The teachers also leveraged and connected the students in their schools and in the participating Finnish schools. Including students in the change process is significant because they are the focus of all educational change initiatives, yet frequently their voices and views are sidelined. In Ian's school, involving students in the conversation is an attempt to let them to play a more active role in the learning process, and an indication that they are part of the community. It is the distributive feature of educational leadership, one that includes all voices, especially those who typically have the least power over *what* is learned, *how* it is learned, and what school *should* be.

Finally, FINAL, as an integrating network, is a significant investment in human and social capital. As Jean shared, a significant learning point from leadership gleaned from the Finnish system is that teachers, by the length of their stay in a school, provide the foundation for the building of bonds, links, and ties within the school community, and the community in which it is located. The apparently conservative nature of Finnish society—with little mobility across schools in the course of one's career—paradoxically enables educators to get to know their students and their families better and to provide a solid foundation for democratic participation and social cohesion. The Finnish emphasis on stability in terms of school staff develops, nurtures, and strengthens ties and links with the community that students enter when they leave school. Stability in schooling then allows external relationships with businesses, government agencies, and nonprofit groups to solidify rather than to change every few years. This is exemplified in the networks that Finnish teachers have established with entrepreneurs and industry that have made their approach to vocational programs such a significant learning experience for the Albertan educators.

Conclusion

As an integrating network, FINAL is still in its nascent stages. This partnership is unique in that the movement provides a way for principals, teachers, and students to experience and learn from another across educational jurisdictions to adapt practices with the collegial support of colleagues from quite different cultural, historical, linguistic, and educational backgrounds. The approach is bottom-up and side-to-side, with leadership throughout exercised by the professionals themselves. Given the predominance of high-powered policy groups to set the international agenda and in many ways to circumvent the professionals who actually are engaged with students on a daily basis, FINAL provides a promising and inspirational counter-narrative, with much value for others who seek not only high educational outcomes, but also humanistic educational processes as part of the path to a better future for all.

References

Bernstein, B. (1975). *Towards a theory of educational transmissions (Vol. 3)*. London: Routledge & Kegan Paul.

Hargreaves, A. (1994). *Changing teachers, changing times*. New York: Teachers College Press.

Hargreaves, A., & Fink, D. (2006). *Sustainable leadership*. San Francisco: Jossey Bass/Wiley.

Hargreaves, A., & Shirley, D. (2009). *The fourth way: The inspiring future for educational change*. Thousand Oaks, CA: Corwin.

Human Resources and Skills Development Canada. (2012). Learning: School drop-outs. Retrieved 15 February, 2012, from http://www4.hrsdc.gc.ca/.3ndic.1t.4r@-eng.jsp?iid=32

Lee, H. L. (2004, November 20, 2008). National Day Rally 2004 Speech, Sunday, 22 August 2004, at the University Cultural Centre, National University of Singapore. Retrieved 10

September, 2011, from http://www.getforme.com/pressreleases/leehl_220804_nationaldayrally2004.htm

Linnakyla, P., & Malin, A. (2008). Finnish students' school engagement profiles in the light of PISA 2003. *Scandinavian Journal of Educational Research, 52*(6), 583-602.

Lortie, D. C. (1975). *Schoolteacher: A sociological study.* Chicago, IL.: University of Chicago Press.

Maslow, A. (1954). *Motivation and personality.* New York: Harper.

Sahlberg, P. (2011). *Finnish lessons: What can the world learn from educational change in Finland?* New York: Teachers College Press.

Shanmugaratnam, T. (2005, 2 January 2008). Achieving quality: Bottom up initiative, top down support. Speech by Mr Tharman Shanmugaratnam, Minister for Education, at the MOE Work Plan Seminar 2005, on Thursday, 22 September 2005. Retrieved 20 November, 2008, from http://www.moe.gov.sg/media/speeches/2005/sp20050922.htm

Stiles, J. (2011). Creating a great school for all students. *ATA Magazine, 92*(2), 32-33. Willms, J. D. (2003). Student engagement at school: A sense of belonging and participation (Results from PISA 2000) Retrieved from http://www.oecd.org/dataoecd/42/35/33689437.pdf

World Health Organization. (2001-2002). Young people's health in context. Health behavior in school-aged children study: International report from the 2001/2 survey. Retrieved 1

February, 2012, from
http://www.hbsc.org/downloads/IntReport04/Part1.pdf

World Health Organization. (2005-2006). Inequalities in young people's health. Health behavior in school-aged children: International report from the 2005/2006 survey. Retrieved 1 February, 2012, from http://www.euro.who.int/__data/assets/pdf_file/0005/53852/E91416.pdf

(Re)Thinking Leadership in a Digital Age: Perspectives, Provocations and Actions
Philip McRae

Will every child in the future have a computer, but only the privileged have a teacher?

Introduction

The world's education systems are in the midst of change (aka 'informed transformation'), unlike any we have seen over the past century. It's a historical moment where governments, teachers, principals, parents, and school communities are exploring visions of an education system that would embody innovation (technologies and pedagogy), increased flexibility (curricular and otherwise), and more individualized and self-directed approaches to student learning. Within this 21st-century tsunami of change, innovative teaching and learning practices that employ emerging technologies are sweeping into our collective imaginations with the broader goal of transforming education. Too often, however, the space for dialogue about the opportunities and challenges of emerging technologies is non-existent, superficial or uninformed, so more thoughtful considerations never surface.

This chapter is meant to share some of the evolving perspectives, provocations, and actions for school leadership around innovation, technology and educational practice. It begins by exploring what leadership looks like in times of rapid technological shift, and how our previous scholarship on shared and distributed leadership structures can be instructive as we move into the future. It continues with some of the philosophical tensions and provocations around 'technology', and how our perspectives shape our actions. Finally, we close with some inquiries that frame the over-arching purposes for learning and technology in our society.

Leadership from the Inside Out

Leadership has traditionally been described through separate definitions or approaches (Leithwood & Duke, 1999; Yukl, 2002), many of which are often combined and discussed based on the contextual setting. The six major definitions of school leadership that dominate the literature tend to be:

1. instructional, transformational
2. moral
3. participatory (i.e., distributed and democratic)
4. managerial
5. contingency (i.e., situational and style) approaches (Leithwood & Duke, 1999)

It is, however, most commonly defined as a process whereby influence is exerted by one person (or group) over other people (or groups) in an effort to structure and facilitate activities and relationships within a school or district (Yukl, 2002). Along with a small handful of personal 'traits' such as optimism, perseverance, flexibility and open-mindedness; the crucial factor in the scholarship around the principal as 'leader' appears to be the individual's determination and ability to create space and encourage relationships (from the inside-out) between teachers and the principal.

Participatory (i.e., distributed) and situational leadership that is focused on building internal leadership capacity in teachers and the local community is the foundation of innovative education systems. It is sustainable, dynamic, energetic and efficacious. Longitudinal research on the Alberta Initiative for School Improvement (AISI) demonstrates this time and again, and shows that educational successes arise through a blend of formal leadership and more distributed and informal forms of leadership enacted in professional learning communities (McRae & Parsons, 2007). These professional learning communities are often characterized by a shared "mission, vision and values; collective inquiry; collaborative teams; an orientation toward action and a willingness to experiment; commitment to continuous improvement; and a focus on results" (DuFour & Eaker, 1998, p. 45).

Leadership in a Digital Age

Distributed leadership has led many professional learning communities towards 'innovative' instructional strategies, educational practices with technology, and a profound knowledge of the new 21st century environments within which they need to support student learning (Foster, McRae & Wright, 2009). Many schools now engage with different models of collaborative professional learning community as a means for teachers to assume responsibility for initiating, sustaining, and integrating learning and technology initiatives (Parsons, McRae,

& Taylor, 2006). These professional learning communities, when balanced with other demands, have great potential to promote collective learning and build leadership capacity throughout the school community in how to appropriately infuse technologies into the curriculum and pedagogical practices.

However, there is still a place for the school principal to enable the creation of a vision for technology in the learning context. The Principal Quality Practice Guidelines for education in the province of Alberta reflect this desire by stating that principals will "recognize(s) the potential of new and emerging technologies, and enable(s) their meaningful integration in support of teaching and learning" (Alberta Education, 2009, p.5). The critical vehicle to meaningfully infusing technology into any learning context is not the lone, omni-competent technology champion, but shared/distributed leadership models where a broadly established community of learners is engaged in discovery and inquiry together.

Perspectives

Technology should never be considered the principal driver of innovative educational transformation (as technological determinists would suggest), nor just a neutral and innocuous tool (as technological instrumentalists claim). The reality is far more complex and it would serve school leaders well to dig deeper into the dialogue around innovation and emerging technologies in education.

On the more mechanistic side of the conversation, there's the technological deterministic view that sees technology as the primary determinant of human experiences. As Selwyn (2011) notes, technological determinism has influenced discussions about innovative educational change for many years. In their day, filmstrips, radio, and televisions were each characterized as having the power to radically transform public education and offer the most innovative solutions to educational challenges.

In the early 1920s, for example, Thomas Edison predicted that the motion picture was "destined to revolutionize our educational system and...in a few years it will supplant largely, if not entirely, the use of textbooks" (Oppenheimer, 1997). This prediction was followed 40 years later with psychologist B. F. Skinner's assertion that the dawn of the machine age of education had finally arrived and that "with the help of teaching machines and programmed instruction, students could learn twice as much in the same time and with the same effort as in a standard classroom" (Oppenheimer, 1997). Similar claims are now being made for online learning (Christensen, 2011).

The proliferation of motion pictures has not fully withdrawn the desire for educational print, and the teaching machines (whatever you imagine those to be) have not yet displaced the will for teachers and students to gather together to learn in inquiry oriented classrooms. Rarely is the imagined future of innovation accurate; more often than not the predictive space tilts heavily in either an overly optimistic or a deeply pessimistic direction. History offers perspective and provides us with at least two important insights: (1) there have always been, and always will be, strong and weak educational practices; and (2) technologies in education, as Selwyn (2011) establishes, rarely live up to the utopian forecasts of their most enthusiastic advocates.

At the other end of the spectrum lives the more common technological instrumentalists' deception, which suggests that technology is just a "tool"; an innocent object; value-free and in the service of whatever subjective goals we chose to ascribe the device. According to this view, technology is culturally neutral and innocuous (Kelly 2005; Levy 2001). Such a view ignores Marshall McLuhan's (1964) caution that, just as we shape our technologies, so they subsequently shape our habits of mind and physical selves.

As educators champion the visible promise of technology to engage students and enhance their learning experiences, it must be recognized that technology is not neutral, nor is it "just a tool". As we enter the year 2020, students and teachers will be immersed in a world where online (silicon)/offline (carbon) boundaries will have blurred to non-existence and where we will be supported by machines talking to machines. With the explosion of digital connectivity "everyware", students, teachers, educational administrators, and parents will be able to access the information they want – how they want it, when they want it and where they want it (think: any time, any place or any pace).

The contemporary World Wide Web is rapidly moving toward what Sir Tim Berners-Lee has called the "Semantic Web" (Berners-Lee 1999; Berners-Lee, Hendler & Lassila 2001). Berners-Lee, the chief architect and creator of the World Wide Web, has been working on the next generation of the Internet at MIT for over a decade. He has articulated his vision for the Semantic Web as follows:

> I have a dream for the Web...[Computers] become capable of analyzing all the data on the Web – the content, links, and transactions between people and computers. A "Semantic Web," which should make this possible, has yet to emerge, but when it does, the day-to-day mechanisms of trade, bureaucracy, and our daily lives will be handled by machines talking to machines. ... The intelligent "agents" people have touted for ages will finally materialize (Berners-Lee 1999, 157–58).

The future of the Internet would then appear to be a technological perfection, where students could create knowledge tailored to their specific interests and ideological orientations. This will have a profound effect on critical thinking as children and youth are increasingly fed only the exact type of information (specific political views, topical book themes, local environmental conditions) and sources (individual blogs, mainstream media online, ethnically oriented Web spaces) to which they subscribe.

In many ways, this personalized (customized) digital state is already in its infancy: consider the highly accurate book recommendations (based on purchasing habits) from Amazon and RSS (Really Simple Syndication), which deliver (feeds) information updates from select Web sites to a personalized Web portal. This active screening of content, facilitated by the emergent nature of the Semantic Web, is a state that Nicholas

Negroponte (1995), former director of the MIT Media Lab and chairman of the global One Laptop Per Child Initiative, has dubbed the "Daily Me."

As students engage in a blurred online/offline reality, with only the content that they want to see, hear and read about, notions of diversity will be increasingly challenged, while free will and personal choice will take on new (and obscured) meanings in these echo chambers (McRae, 2007, 2011a). The echo-chamber effect is a condition arising in an online community where participants find their own opinions constantly echoed back to them, thus reinforcing their individual belief systems. Participants within online collaborative spaces will always act in human ways: that is, people will gravitate toward and be more comfortable communicating with those who share their ideas, conceptions of the truth, cultures and communication styles (McRae, 2007).

In considering this long-term trend, educators need to be thoughtful about the role of critical thinking, diversity and chance; their importance to learning and society, and the long-term implications of driving digital personalization (customization) within our educational discourse. For school leaders, identifying the challenge of the digital 'echo-chamber effect' to the role of critical thinking in our educational environments will soon become even more critical.

Provocations

Emerging technologies are paradoxical in that they hold both promise and peril for individuals, families and communities. At a time of rapid technological change, school leaders working with children, families, schools, and communities need to understand the impact of online digital activities for offline health and mental wellbeing.

Adults have more choice than do children with respect to how they consume technologies. Furthermore, children's bodies, which are still developing, are more susceptible to the potential harmful effects of technology than are those of adults. For this reason, teachers need to better understand how spending long periods of time in front of a computer screen can affect children and youth. Although research on this topic is still in its infancy, studies have already shown, for example, that playing violent video games can make children more aggressive; that sitting for long periods in front of a computer can contribute to obesity; that excessive gaming and Internet use can interfere with children's psychosocial wellbeing, diminish their attention spans, and contribute to vision problems; and that using technology in the evening can disrupt children's sleep patterns and have related consequences (Howard-Jones, 2011; Canadian Paediatric Society, 2009).

There is a growing call for studies on the physiological effect of digital technologies and new media on children's brain development—a neuroscience of children and media (Anderson, 2007). Based on this concern, educators should carefully consider the personal cost to 8–18-year-olds who average 10 hours and 45 minutes a day per day exposed to media (Kaiser Foundation, 2010), or the Canadian Paediatric Society's recent policy recommendation of no screen time for children under two years of age, and a maximum of two hours for children older than two (Canadian Paediatric Society, 2009). Issues engendered by the pervasive digital connectivity of young people and society are critical if schools as hubs in the community hope to promote a healthy, balanced society.

Finally, we should be mindful of saving stillness in a digital age; where a kind of solitude from technology - that refreshes and restores a person - is valued. Stillness is a particular concern that distinguished professor Sherry Turkle, director of MIT Initiative on Technology and Self, argues is essential to identity formation and healthy adolescent development in the 21st century. Turkle speculates that, "If we identify our need for stillness as something that is part of our human purposes, we will find ways to bring it back into our lives. If we only get excited about what technology makes easy, we will say that this is a kind of…18th century completely passé thing and that it is not essential. I think that part of K–12 education now should be to give students a place for this kind of stillness, because I don't think that the rest of their lives is making it easy for them" (Dretzin 2009).

Teaching and Learning with Technology

Educators should constantly be reflecting on how digital technologies are pragmatically being integrated into classrooms to enhance learning, and what impact the media is playing on the teacher-student relationship. The Media Awareness Network (MNet) completed an enlightening Canadian study on how digital technologies are being infused into kindergarten to grade

12 classrooms, how they enhance learning, and what effect digital media is having on teacher-student relationships (MNet, 2012).

In this work, MNet notes that teachers' impressions of students' abilities with (and knowledge of) digital media are most often incorrect. As a teacher participant in the study from Atlantic Canada said: "I don't think students are all that Internet-savvy. I think they limit themselves to very few tools on the Internet. They're locked into using it in particular ways and don't think outside the box ... I'm always surprised at the lack of knowledge that students have about how to search and navigate online" (MNet, 2012, p. 9).

Teachers in the MNet (2012) study identified several obstacles (not in any particular order of priority) to infusing technology into learning:

1. Internet filters and bans on personal digital devices such as tablets and Smartphones.
2. Pressure to teach technical skills instead of digital literacy skills.
3. Potential for digital technologies to cause disruptions in the classroom.
4. Shortage of professional learning opportunities on technology integration.

Despite the above obstacles, respondents overwhelmingly noted that digital media provide tremendous opportunities for teachers and students, as long as students can engage critically with media and consider the ethical ramifications of what they do online. As one elementary teacher put it, "The biggest skill students need is a moral compass" (MNet, 2012, p. 22).

A priority consideration, then, for teaching and learning with technology in a digital age should be supporting students with digital literacy and citizenship skills in their classrooms and schools, across grade levels and disciplines. Teachers should spend little (or no time) focusing on how to use the "tool"; instead, they should teach students how to appropriately access, create, critique, understand and use technology.

Challenges of Cost, Complexity, Access and Support

There are many contradictions and paradoxes around emerging technologies in support of teaching and learning. A sea of questions constantly ebbs and flows for educators around how to effectively and efficiently navigate the costs, complexities, access, and supports required to place information and communication technologies into the numerous imaginative learning scenarios put forward by parent communities, superintendents, students, and teachers.

Costs

Questions of financial (and indeed human) costs and efficiency should weigh heavily on school leaders as they consider the scope of technology purchases among the many other competing priorities in a school.

School jurisdictions have made significant investments of capital (both human and financial) and technology-use resources in an attempt to enhance learning and solve complex problems. These investments primarily consist of time, energy, attention, and money that can detract from other facets of a full and inclusive public education system. A learning context should engage technology, but also achieve a fine balance between arts-based curriculum, supports for English language learners, cares for special needs students, involvement in community-oriented sports and recreational programs, and enrichment of the school by teacher librarians, nurses, and career and guidance counselors.

Far too often, the shiny object of technology is given more prestige than it deserves. The release of Apple's digital textbooks in 2012 had technocrats and technophiles hailing the arrival of educational transformation. *"Apple And The Coming Education Revolution"*, blared the headline at Fast Company magazine. *"Apple puts iPad at head of the class"*, screamed MacWorld. And Time magazine declared the announcement the *"debut (of) the holy grail of textbooks"* (Sirota, 2012). Yet when more thoughtfully considered, it is recognized that the costs of a non-transferrable digital textbook may only be in the double digits, but the perpetual content updates and ever greening costs of the hardware will eventually devour the school budget.

School leadership must carefully determine the needs of children and youth and the values of the community before identifying the priority actions that will be addressed to meet these needs. As Murgatroyd and Couture (ATA, 2010) would suggest, attempting to implement technology without first taking into account other changes - an increasingly diverse student population, integrated classrooms, and the decline in rural populations - is to put the cart before the horse. Although technology must be part of the educational support for students, it cannot be rationally placed as the prime investment for education.

Complexity

The most challenging systemic issues reside in larger complexities and include: poverty and inequity across a society; a lack of parental engagement (or conversely hyper-parenting); large class sizes; and complex compositions that impede more personalized learning experiences. All of these are bound up in numerous digital and popular culture distractions that impact children's readiness to learn. When implementing technology, pedagogical leaders should take into account these many complexities, including diverse factors such as the age, gender and education level of students, the socioeconomic status of the community, and the beliefs that a student's parents and peers hold about the value of technology both in and outside a school setting (McRae, 2011b).

Another complexity of pervasive technology access is information overload. As the cost of technology has declined, the volume of information and the number of services that it is capable of delivering have increased exponentially. In the past, most economic 'laws' have been premised on the principle that resources are finite. By contrast, some commentators have characterized the proliferation of information that technology has made possible as an example of the "economics of abundance". But as *Wired* editor-in-chief Chris Anderson (Anderson, 2005) observes, "although there may be near infinite selection of all media, there is still a scarcity of human attention and hours in the day." In essence, "scarcity bottlenecks" have shifted "from the CPU to the user." It seems we are still faced with limitations, after all.[25]

Access

Teachers, students and families do not necessarily have equitable access to technology. Wealthy schools and school authorities that can implement economies of scale are much more likely to benefit from technology than smaller rural schools, many of which struggle to find the learning and human resources they need to use advanced technology, even when the hardware and infrastructures are in place (Looker & Thiessen, 2003).

It is easy to be seduced by the appearance of abundance. In reality, what we are facing is a world of infinite choice and infinite information (think echo-chamber effect), and yet we still have to decide how to use all this information. Psychologist Barry Schwartz (Schwartz, 2004) has called this phenomenon the "tyranny of choice", pointing out that more choice can lead to paralyzing indecision, anxiety and decreased wellness. Because technology can greatly increase the choices available, it is not surprising that work intensification is more likely to occur in

---

[25]Classical economic theory is rooted in the notion of scarcity: unlimited wants and needs in a world of finite resources. Theoretically, digitized information constitutes an "infinite" resource. For more, see Anderson (2005).

information-rich work environments (Chung-Yan, 2010; Green, 2004).

Technology has made it easier for teachers to produce student achievement data. In many school jurisdictions, teachers are using student achievement data - not only for reporting purposes, but also to improve their practice and enhance their communications with parents. This situation is a good example of how the ability to produce nearly unlimited data can surpass the finite time and energy that teachers (or students and parents) have to consume this data. Hargreaves and Shirley (2009) describe this scenario as a distracting path of technocracy, in which the capacity to produce data outstrips the critical skills and time that people have to evaluate the data and use it meaningfully.

Support
One of the most significant challenges for both teachers and school principals is how to respond to the many demands from teacher colleagues and students for access to various software resources, new "add on" technologies or apps for Smartphone and tablet devices. A lack of technology and restricted access (because of filtering and firewalls) often limits an educator's ability to make appropriate decisions. As well, many teachers and school leaders do not often receive the professional development they need to use technology in a way that fully supports student learning. Teachers and principals also need mentors who can help bring digital media into learning contexts in appropriate and pedagogically powerful ways, particularly

considering the shortage of professional development time and resources in most school communities. Finding ways to support professional learning experiences that directly address their unique learning and technology concerns (more personalized professional learning) is a major factor in enhancing a teacher's digital literacy and sense of efficacy around emerging technologies (ATA, 2011).

Another challenge is the false distinction made between the teacher or school principal being a digital "immigrant" while the students are to be regarded as digital '"natives" (Prensky, 2001). This trope has become common in the field of education and broader cultural contexts, as a way of framing the rapid technological changes which are reshaping our learning communities in a digital age. These notions are often sourced as a rationale for why young teachers are better positioned to infuse technology into the classrooms.

The concern over whether teachers are digital immigrants or natives is a common distraction. The critical factors to successful technology infusion are a teacher's pedagogical experience, deep curricular knowledge and effective classroom management skills, as opposed to their age or 'savvy' knowledge of technology. These attributes give educators the freedom to take chances, and enable students to be leaders and design new ways of engaging with technologies. In other words, it is not about the age of the teacher or principal, it is more about their experience and craft knowledge.

Taking Action: Phronesis

As school leaders determine a practical starting point for enhancing educational practices through the use of digital technologies, phronetic action, as articulated by Flyvbjerg (2004), might inform this undertaking. Phronesis is an Aristotelian consideration that has been translated to mean 'contextualized' practical wisdom. As Eisner (2002) suggests, the term *phronesis* refers to wise practical reasoning, and is "deliberative, it takes into account local circumstances, it weighs tradeoffs, it is riddled with uncertainties, it depends upon judgment, profits from wisdom, addresses particulars, it deals with contingencies, is iterative and shifts aims in process when necessary. Practical reasoning is the stuff of practical life" (p. 375). he very purpose of phronetic action is to clarify the specific values, interests and power relations in any given situation, and then consider these in light of potential actions, problems and risks that are to be faced in a certain domain of pedagogic action.

Several value-rational questions for phronetic social action can be adapted for school leaders to posit and answer as they employ their judgment regarding the place of technologies in learning. The purpose of these questions for phronetic action is to clarify where educators are in their practice, where they might want to go in light of technology's affordances (and seductions), and what is deemed desirable according to the very contextualized and diverse sets of values and interests that school leadership must balance:

   1. Where are schools going in a globalized and digital era?

2. Who gains and who loses as students engage with digital technologies?
3. By which mechanisms of power is this activity mediated?
4. When is learning with technology a desirable action?
5. What, if anything, should educators do about it?

The "we" in these questions always refers to a very specific learning context and, as noted earlier in this chapter, should be distributed and shared across the education community at large. School leaders should deliberate over these questions and, in doing so, reach beyond analytical, epistemic, and technical knowledge. This should involve judgments and decisions in a way that supports a participatory pedagogy around technology as one of many ways to enhance teaching and learning.

Taking Action: Technological Pedagogical Content Knowledge (TPACK)

In assessing how digital technologies might be used appropriately to engender more innovative learning experiences, educators might consider using the well-conceived Technological Pedagogical Content Knowledge (TPACK) model (Koehler and Mishra 2009). TPACK tries to reconcile the complexity and dynamics of student learning as it relates to technology and the multifaceted nature of teachers' knowledge. Rather than conceptualizing content knowledge (CK), pedagogical knowledge (PK) and technology knowledge (TK) as isolated entities, TPACK focuses on the interplay between these knowledge sources. TPACK asks educators to consider how the various knowledge sources apply to a particular learning situation. No single pedagogical approach applies to every teacher or every student. The teacher must traverse the elements of content, pedagogy and technology, and understand how they interact in the context of learning. A more thorough explanation of TPACK can be found in the thoughtful work of Koehler and Mishra (2009).

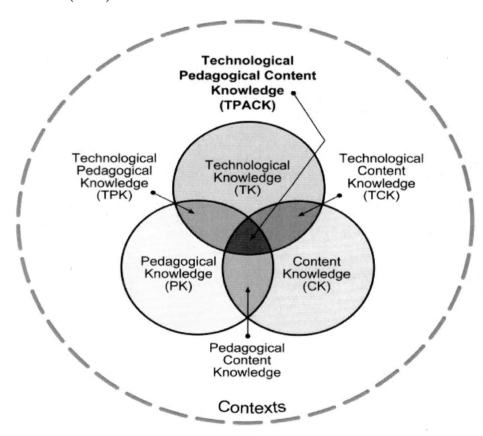

The TPACK Model (Koehler and Mishra, 2009)

Conclusion

Innovative teaching and learning with technology is a dynamic, challenging and creative act, and if we are to (re)think leadership in a digital age, we must remember that it can never reside in just one person given the complexity of our times. Rethinking leadership in relation to learning and technology means conceptualizing school leadership as distributed and shared between many individuals and communities. It means school leaders have a strong sense of efficacy related to learning and technology decisions, and are continually able to explore both the promise and perils of a technology enhanced environment.

For the skilled pedagogical leaders, an ancient perspective must rise up and demand that the education of our next generations should not be about machines (videoconferencing, laptops and personal owned devices and learning objects), but rather, a community of learners whose physical, intellectual and social well-being is held sacred. This point of view is driven by the human desire to connect, maintain friendships, tell stories, share thoughts and inquire into the nature of the world.

It is a perspective that naturally flows together with research on learning that suggests that education is not just about content or physical place, but also a collective and highly relational set of experiences within a community of learners. In the research on education, learning is successful when it is socially constructed, and occurs in an active and inquiry-oriented process that engages people in social, emotional, cultural, and deeply intrapersonal experiences. This research will likely hold true whether our future learning environments are enacted face to face, online, or in blended learning online/offline contexts as this carbon and silicon line begins to blur. It also holds true regardless of whether one is considered digitally literate, or a member of the New Millennial Generation (Gen M).

As educators swim in a sea of emerging technologies and envision their power to transform our public education system, we must embrace this historical moment as an opportunity to discuss how we want to live together in the future and to identify the attributes that are needed to flourish as a society. As communities of learners help students become creative and innovative individuals capable of participating in diverse and complex communities, two questions should call out for school leadership:

1. *How might school leaders engage with digital technologies so that they help students become empowered citizens, rather than passive consumers?*
2. *What technological experiences will help students create a future where we can all flourish within informed, democratic, and diverse communities; as opposed to fashioning a hyper-digitized society of narcissists that are fragmented by a continuous partial attention?*

References

Alberta Education (2009). *Principal Quality Practice Guidelines*. Edmonton, AB: Government of Alberta. Retrieved January 12, 2012 from http://education.alberta.ca/media/949129/principal-quality-practice-guideline-english-12feb09.pdf

Alberta Teachers' Association (ATA) (2010). *Using Technology to Put Real Learning First in Alberta Schools*. Edmonton, AB: Alberta Teachers' Association. Retrieved January 24, 2012 from http://www.teachers.ab.ca/SiteCollectionDocuments/ATA/Publications/Research-Updates/PD-86-17%20Using%20Technology%20to%20Support%20RLF%20in%20Alberta%20Schools.pdf

Alberta Teachers' Association (ATA), (2011). *The Impact of Digital Technologies on Teachers Working in Flexible Learning Environments* Edmonton, AB: Alberta Teachers' Association. Retrieved February 24, 2012 from http://www.teachers.ab.ca/SiteCollectionDocuments/ATA/Publications/Research-Updates/PD-86-21%20Impact%20of%20Digital%20Technologies.pdf

Anderson, C.A. (2007). A neuroscience of children and media? *Journal of Children and Media* 1, no. 1: 77–85.

Anderson, C. (2005). The tragically neglected economics of abundance. *The Long Tail*. Retrieved December 14, 2012 from http://longtail.typepad.com/the_long_tail/2005/03/the_tragically_.html.

Berners-Lee, T. (1999). *Weaving the web: The original design and ultimate destiny of the world wide web by its inventor*. San Francisco: HarperSanFrancisco.

Berners-Lee, T., J. Hendler & Lassila. O. (2001). The semantic web. *Scientific American* 284 (May): 34–43.

Canadian Paediatric Society (2009). *Impact of media use on children and youth*. Ottawa, ON: Canadian Paediatric Society. Retrieved December 19, 2012 from www.cps.ca/english/statements/CP/pp03-01.htm#RECOMMENDATIONS

Christensen, C. (2011) Why Online Education is Ready for Disruption, Now. Available at http://thenextweb.com/insider/2011/11/13/clayton-christensen-why-online-education-is-ready-for-disruption-now/

Chung-Yan, G. (2010). The nonlinear effects of job complexity and autonomy on job satisfaction: Turnover and psychological wellbeing. *Journal of Occupational Health Psychology* 15(3), 237-51.

Dretzin, R. (2009, September 22). *Interview with Sherry Turkle*. Frontline.

Dufour, R., & Eaker, R. (1998). *Professional learning communities at work: Best practices for enhancing student achievement*. Bloomington, Indiana: National Educational Service.

Flyvbjerg, B. (2004). Phronetic planning research: Theoretical and methodological reflections. *Journal of Planning Theory & Practice*, (5), 283–306.

Foster, R., McRae, P. & Wright, L. (2009). Leading and sustaining school improvement initiatives.

Research paper presentation for the Canadian Association for the Study of Educational Administration (CASEA) at the annual conference of the Canadian Society for the Study of Education (CSSE), Ottawa, ON: CSSE

Green, F. (2004). "Work Intensification, Discretion and the Decline in Wellbeing at Work." *Eastern Economic Journal* 30(4): 615–26.

Hargreaves, A, & Shirley, D. (2009). *The Fourth Way – The Inspiring Future for Educational Change*. Thousand Oaks, CA: Corwin.

Howard-Jones, P. (2011). *The Impact of Digital Technologies on Human Wellbeing: Evidence from the Sciences of Mind and Brain*. Oxford, England: Nominet Trust.

Kelly, K. (2005). We Are the web. *Wired Magazine* (8)13. Available at http://www.wired.com/wired/archive/13.08/tech.html (accessed June 14, 2011).

Kaiser Family Foundation (2010). Generation M2: Media in the Lives of 8–18 Year Olds. Menlo Park, CA: Henry J. Kaiser Family Foundation.

Koehler, M.J., & Mishra, P. (2009). "What Is Technological Pedagogical Content Knowledge?" *Contemporary Issues in Technology and Teacher Education* 9(1): 60–70.

Levy, P. (2001). *Cyberculture*. Minneapolis: University of Minnesota Press.

Leithwood, K., & Duke, D. (1999). A century's quest to understand school leadership. In J. Murphy & K. Seashore Louis (Eds.), *Handbook of research on educational* administration *(2nd ed.)*, (pp. 45-72). San Francisco, CA: Jossey-Bass.

Looker, D, & Thiessen, V. (2003). *The Digital Divide in Canadian Schools: Factors Affecting Student Access to and Use of Information Technology*. Ottawa, ON: Statistics Canada. Also available at http://www.statcan.gc.ca/pub/81-597-x/81-597-x2003001-eng.pdf (accessed November 9, 2011).

McLuhan, M. (1964). *Understanding Media*. New York: Mentor.

McRae, P. (2007). *Argumentum ad infinitum: The complex nature of echoing voices on the Internet.* Research paper presentation at the Complexity Science and Educational Research (CSER) conference, Vancouver, BC: University of British Columbia.

McRae, P. (2011a). *Forecasting the Future Over Three Horizons of Change*. Media Awareness Network of Canada. National Media Literacy Week Press Kit. Ottawa, ON: MNet.

McRae, P. (2011b). Yong Zhao: Catching up or leading the way: American education in the age of globalization. *Journal of Educational Change*. 1(12). Netherlands: Springer, p. 1389-2843.

McRae, P., & Parsons, J. (2007). *Systemic school improvement - Key findings from six years with the Alberta initiative for school improvement*. Research roundtable for Canadian Association for

Teacher Education (CATE) at the annual conference of the Canadian Society for the Study of Education (CSSE), Saskatoon, SK: CSSE.

MNet (2012). *Young Canadians in a wired world, phase III: Teachers' perspectives.* Accessed online March 20, 2012 at http://media-awareness.ca/english/corporate/media_kit/upload/YCWW-III-Teachers-Perspectives_EN.pdf

Negroponte, N. (1995). *Being Digital.* New York: Knopf. Oppenheimer, T. (1997). The computer delusion. *Atlantic Monthly* 280, no 1 (July): 45–62.

Parsons, J., McRae, P., & Taylor, L. (2006). Celebrating school improvement: Six lessons learned from Alberta's AISI projects (2nd edition). Edmonton, AB: School Improvement Press, 190 pages. ISBN #: 1-55220-053-1

Prensky, M. (2001). Digital natives, Digital immigrants. *On the Horizon*, Vol. 9 No. 5, University of Nebraska: NCB University Press.

Schwartz, B. (2004). The tyranny of voice. *Scientific American Magazine* (April 2004, 71–75).

Eisner, E. (2002). From episteme to phronesis to artistry in the study and improvement of teaching. *Teaching and Teacher Education, (18)*, 375 - 385.

Selwyn, N. (2011). *Schools and schooling in the digital Age: A critical analysis.* London and New York: Routledge.

Sirota, D. (2012, February 3). *Are high-tech classrooms better classrooms?* Salon.com Accessed March 10, 2012 http://www.salon.com/2012/02/03/are_high_tech_classrooms_better_classrooms

Wilson, F. (2006). *My favorite business model.* AVC A VC in NYC: March 23, 2006 blog posting. Accessed January 23, 2012 http://avc.blogs.com/a_vc/2006/03/my_favorite_bus.html

Yukl, G. (2002). *Leadership in organizations (5th ed.).* Upper Saddle, NJ: Prentice Hall.

The School as a Centre for Perpetual Innovation
Stephen Murgatroyd, PhD, FBPsS, FRSA

Introduction

The term "innovation" is widely misunderstood. It is often confused with research and development (R&D), for example. Both research and development can be helpful in the context of innovation, but they are often unnecessary. This is because a great deal of innovation is "adopt and adapt" – taking an idea from one sector or jurisdiction, modifying it and then applying the idea in a different sector or jurisdiction. One example of this is taking the idea of using technology enabled learning to provide open schooling in former commonwealth countries which have poor performing K-12 systems. The Commonwealth of Learning, established in 1995, is in part dedicated to open schooling and is making this happen on a large scale[i].

Another form of innovation is disruptive. This occurs when someone has a breakthrough idea or understanding that fundamentally changes how something gets done. Commercial aircraft, once seen as an impossibility, were a breakthrough. Hand held Smartphones for mobile learning could well become a breakthrough. The development of stem cell based treatments for cancer is disruptive. Many of these require more research and development than adopt and adapt innovations, but the R&D component is a small part of the process. The real work is taking a basic idea from a laboratory or workbench or idea club and making it work on a large scale, repeatedly at a reasonable or lower cost in comparison with current practice.

Innovation is a process which can be taught and developed, both to individuals and to organizations. It requires a disciplined approach to change and effective leadership, but it also requires sensing, envisioning and engaging – all creative processes which teachers are required to do every day in their classrooms – skills on which they can build for effective innovation aimed at significant performance improvement.

In this chapter, the eight practices of innovation are outlined and described together with the leadership requirements for each practice. The focus is on within school innovation and the power of communities of practice, whether the focus is on curriculum, teaching and learning processes, school administration and management or community partnerships and alliances. The purpose of the chapter is to provide a framework for a conversation about what a school is doing to make itself a centre for perpetual innovation.

Making Innovation Happen – What is Innovation?

A lot of time has been wasted in writing, researching and thinking about innovation and developing "innovation systems". Few work. For example, the U.S. Patents Office reports that less than 0.2% of patents actually produce a return on the investment made in patenting – most are worth considerably less (if anything) than the cost of protecting the patent. While governments make massive investments in innovation – the Government of Canada, for example, invests some $14 billion a year – most of this goes into R&D. Yet we also know that fewer than 25% of all innovative products and services can be traced back to any specific R&D. From a practical business perspective, less than 4% of corporate innovations meet their financial objectives or produce the returns on investment or capital employed promised by the proponents of the innovation[ii]. Innovation is a risky, messy process. This messiness arises because of the confusion of thinking about what innovation is.

So let us define innovation in a way that makes sense for schools. *Innovation is the adoption of practices (ways of working, thinking and behaving) within a community we call school that has an impact on outcomes*. There are some key elements of this definition. The first is *community*. This refers to any group of more than two people. In a school, it could be the Modern Language team, all Grade 3 teachers or another group. In a District it could be all elementary schools, all Mathematics Teachers, all High School Principals or another grouping. The key is that a community of people act collectively to make a difference in an agreed way.

The second key work is *practice*. By this we mean the habits, routines, approaches, ways of working, or behaviour that members of the community engage in frequently. Effective innovation leads this community to engage in innovative practice without conscious thought – it becomes their second nature.

The final key word in this definition of innovation is *adoption*. The new practice, soon to become an unconscious way of doing things within the community, is consciously chosen and put to use because it makes a difference to some chosen outcome. These outcomes can be behavioural (better behaved students), educational (improved understanding of difficult content, improved performance on assessments, higher levels of student engagement), social (better teamwork or higher levels of student engagement) or cultural (building a culture of creativity, unleashing imaginations). Effective educational innovation is thus not just good ideas adopted by one teacher, it has to make a difference to some outcome for a community and has to change some aspect of practice and have an impact on outcomes.

Making Innovation Happen – Eight Processes for Invention, Adoption and Sustaining Next Practice

So what does it take to make innovation happen in a school?

There are a variety of descriptions of the work of schools as innovation centres, some of which were documented in *Total Quality Management and the School*[iii] and others have provided more specific reviews of innovation processes in education[iv]. What follows here is based on Denning and Dunham's work[v], adapted for schools. They identify eight core practices that make innovation as defined here a sustaining change in how a school or an organization undertakes its work. These eight processes are outlined in the table below. They look neat and tidy in this table, but, in fact, the work of innovation is..

The Eight Innovation Processes			
The Work of Invention	1	Sensing	Sensing that there is an opportunity to undertake things differently - looking and seeing what others are doing, engaging with others in different parts of the world, taking a note of developments in other sectors (e.g. health, non profits, business)…Sensing also that there is a need to do something differently…that we could do better. *Developing the sense of knowing*.
	2	Envisioning	Being able to share a compelling story about doing things differently – "selling" a vision, opportunity and showing "how" it works for you with passion. *Showing the courage of conviction*.
The Work of Adoption	3	Offering	Making the offer to work to change an outcome by using the process/work shared in the envisioning process. *Showing the courage of the offer*.
	4	Adopting	Overcoming resistance to

			change by doing what you said you would do with the new process/work and continually improving what you do to produce improved outcomes. *Showing resilience.*
	5	Sustaining	Gaining commitment to keep doing the "new" work and securing the support of one or more first follower. *Showing determination.*
Creating the Environment for Next Practice	6	Executing	Making the "new" way of working routine and effective, such that it produces reliable and consistent improvement in outcomes. *Demonstrating professional effectiveness.*
	7	Leading	Being proactive in mobilizing others within the school (and elsewhere) to adopt the emerging practice and supporting them when their commitment falters or when they need additional support. *Showing professional leadership.*
	8	Embedding	Establish the "new" practice as the norm for

	your school and embody the spirit of "we can change". *Showing that change can work and stick.*

Table 1: Innovative Processes (Derived from Denning and Dunham, 2010)

..messy and uncomfortable. There are many challenges – distrust, doubt, technical difficulties, antagonism, resource constraints amongst them – that have to be overcome. Yet innovation occurs frequently within schools using these kinds of processes.

When we look at specific innovations, they look less linear and more circular – more like the diagram below. In this diagram, all elements are connected and the first two phases are flowing between each other, iteratively and (seemingly) endlessly until the transition is made from the outer work to the inner work of making the innovation stick.

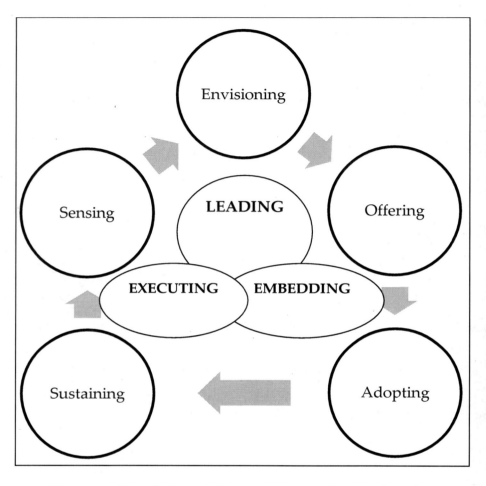

Figure 1: The Ebb and Flow of Innovation In Practice

To put some flesh on this work, let us walk through an innovation example. We use that of a teacher changing the way they ensure students in their Grade 3 class attain reading standards one year in advance of their chronological age initially at a single elementary school in San Francisco (and now, worldwide). We use the table outlined above to provide a short summary of the actions taken by an inspired teacher.

	The Eight Innovation Processes			
The Work of Invention	1	Sensing		Sensing that using technology, community members (especially retirees and grandparents) and developing personalized plans that reflected the interests of each student as well as their current capacity would make a real difference. Reading about other innovations in reading.
	2	Envisioning		Looking at what training coaches, guides and mentors (volunteer helpers) would need so that there was a consistent approach to reading and literacy. Looking at iPad and Smartphone apps that support the strategy. Seeing what it would take to get this scheme to work.
The Work of Adoption	3	Offering		Offering to run a one day course for parents,

			grandparents and those in two seniors' homes to show how they could help make a difference to literacy. Sharing the thinking with the school leadership team and other Grade 3 teachers and securing their support.
	4	Adopting	Securing support from peers, school administration and offering 2 x 1 day courses for coaches, guides and mentors. Working with each child to secure an interest catalogue and developing a personalized reading challenge. Sharing the reading challenges with coaches, mentors and guides. Each child reading to an adult for one hour a day and the adults logging reading strength. Monthly simple assessment. Progress tracking. Hard work – a lot more than anticipated. But results!

	5	Sustaining	Following a presentation to all staff about the work, sharing preliminary results. Securing some resources to continue. Removing opposition to so many "strangers" in the classroom. Tracking not just reading improvement, but behavioural improvement and performance in other subjects and seeing major gains.
Creating the Environment for Next Practice	6	Executing	Developing protocols and rubrics as well as catalogues of apps and tools linked to areas of interests. Increasing the size of the mentor, coach and guide pool and securing the service of all seniors' homes in the district.
	7	Leading	Showcasing outcomes and opportunities at professional development activities across the District. Five other schools follow.

			Now a network of teachers, parents, grandparents and others identifying resources, processes and supports which work.
	8	Embedding	All elementary schools in the district adopt this approach to what is now called Community Based Accelerated Literacy.

Table 2: Case Study of Innovation in Action – Personalizing Literacy and Engaging the Community in the Challenge

Leading for Innovation

We have described a process of innovation and given an example of this process in action. The process focuses on in school innovation, but may also be seen as a model for all innovation activities. The next issue is what does leadership look like within the school to enable such innovation to occur?

There is substantial literature regarding leadership and innovation, little of which is dedicated to looking at the relationship between leadership and innovation in schools or school systems[vi]. But it tends to focus on leaders as the source of innovation. It is more likely, however, especially given the increased qualification of teachers in Canadian schools, that innovation could come from anywhere in the school – from teachers, teacher assistants, students, parents or members of the community. In fact, in the idealized school, this is precisely the point. Innovation comes from the next place it can come from – Principals, Assistant Principals have to be ready.

But what does leadership for "being ready for the next innovation" look like? There are five key components to innovative leadership practice in schools, derived from an extensive review of the school based leadership literature. These are:

1. **Communicating** – Innovative leaders within schools are active listeners, able to facilitate and engage others in focused conversations and challenging dialogues. They are effective at sharing and presenting ideas within the school, community and to organizations. They can speak "truth to power". But they are not over-confident or arrogant. They know how to communicate with respect to co-workers and colleagues and are receptive to sincere advice.
2. **Interpersonal Awareness** - Innovative leaders within schools are emotionally intelligent and have developed a psychological knowledge of those with whom they interact most frequently. They are in control of their emotions, but are able to leverage all aspects of their own psychology in the service of students, the school and the community. They nurture and cherish relationships and can build alliances and partnerships without having to be

at the centre of them. They have a strong service orientation.

3. **Motivating Others** - Innovative leaders within schools are skilled at team building, activity management and enabling others to act within and just beyond their comfort zones. Their interpersonal and communication skills equip them to take charge when they need to do so, but also to be a servant leader when they need to – they use the skills of situational leadership well. They are excellent at reinforcement, encouragement and support.

4. **Developing Others** - Innovative leaders within schools are effective coaches, guides and mentors behaving ethically and with integrity in the development of others. They know how to make processes, activities, knowledge and skills meaningful and accessible and are able to connect these developmental activities to the individuals and teams with which they work. They are skilled at facilitating adult learning. They are also able to quickly assess where others are and where they could be with their coaching and help.

5. **Influencing** - Innovative leaders within schools are politically savvy, empowering and persuasive. They can move an idea through an organization and remove conflicts, road-blocks and negotiate for action. They are inspiring to others, yet modest about themselves. They are co-operators, enablers and doers. Leadership, for them, is not all talk.

Anyone in the school, for the ideas they are passionate about, can be a leader. But they also look to those with positional authority – Principals, Assistant Principals, Departmental leaders – to enable innovation by demonstrating these five practices.

Underlying Leadership Practices of Positional Leaders

School Principalship is widely studied and written about[vii], with a variety of models of instructional leadership and effective or competent management described. Much of this literature mirrors that found in the more general literature of leadership.

Recently, this author has developed a description of renaissance leadership, leveraging the work found in *Renaissance Leadership – Rethinking and Leading the Future*[viii], as applied to education in *Rethinking Education – Learning and the New Renaissance*[ix]. We offer a basic review of this leadership framework since it captures some forty years of work in schools with inspiring educational leaders. Each of these renaissance positional leaders displayed a combination of the six practices described below. But first, context.

Renaissance leaders aren't easily described in a few neat phrases, precisely because they embody the renaissance tendency to break down rigid categories and wander into areas where the industrial mind would say they had no right to be. Consider Leonardo da Vinci, a name often invoked as the quintessential Renaissance Man. Was he a scientist, mathematician, engineer, inventor, anatomist, painter, sculptor, architect, botanist, musician, or writer? Exactly! He was all of these things, and more. Or consider Cosimo de Medici: ambassador, politician, patron of arts and architecture, banker and businessman, founder of a modern Platonic philosophical academy – and one of the lead players in the 15th century Italian Renaissance.

The renaissance leaders were thinkers, but not the type of thinker who prefers the ivory tower and indulges in thought purely for its own sake. They were thinkers with a passion for moving their ideas and knowledge into action. In a similar way, renaissance leaders in the modern knowledge economy are also people of action—but not the ready-fire-aim type of actor who believes that being fast off the mark in implementing the first plan that comes to mind is the key to success. They are self-aware people who pay attention to who they really are - what some might call their "way of being in the world - without descending into self-absorption or losing touch with reality.

They are high integrity individuals with a passion both for driving high performance in their organizations and for helping to make the world a better place.

The modern day Renaissance Leaders have a sense of history and an unusual capacity for viewing the world holistically, for practicing systems thinking, for injecting a global and a futures perspective into present challenges, for honouring diversity, and for drawing on ideas and best practices from diverse disciplines and economic sectors.

They have a capacity to function as social and technical architects designing new structures, processes and products for addressing complex challenges.

They have mastered the art of demonstrating grace under pressure, and of inspiring others to have the courage to collaborate and innovate in order to solve complex challenges.

This is because Renaissance Leaders are role models for other leaders – they have moved from being a good leader to a great leader who inspires others to lead their organizations and communities differently. Renaissance Leaders understand the future and know how they need to lead to make the future a positive one for their organization.

Renaissance Leaders Collaborate

Renaissance Leaders collaborate – they understand that collaboration is the DNA of the knowledge economy. They also understand the range and scope of the collaboration required to build an effective, focused renaissance organization. They seek out:

Collaboration Among People Who Work in the Same School - Because changes are taking place in several areas of a school at the same time, all of which are interrelated, there is a need for collaboration. This is particularly true because leaders are expected to deal with these issues holistically, which means dealing with issues in an integrated fashion. A challenge today in the teaching of science will be a challenge tomorrow in the management of learning.

Collaboration Among Different Schools in the Same Region - Since changes in organizations play themselves out in at least five functional areas of work (Strategy, Structure, Systems, Skills, and

Shared Values), there is an increasing need for collaboration among people from different parts of the school system in a given region. Shared learning; collaboration on cross-school challenges; collaboration on how to leverage IT for improved student performance; all represent samples of the opportunities for system wide collaboration.

Collaboration in Cross Functional Virtual Teams to Run Specific Projects - An elaboration of these two forms of collaboration reminds us that, increasingly, organizations need to put together cross-functional teams to undertake specific tasks. Teams from around the world can now collaborate on projects aimed at improving school performance, as the partnership between schools in Alberta with specific schools in Finland is showing. This collaboration requires a mixed group to learn how to work together efficiently and effectively, quickly and when the task is completed, they go back to their 'normal' work and a new collaborative team is formed to tackle a new task.

Collaboration with Stakeholders and Partners – Increasingly, schools as organizations concentrate on their key competencies which allow them to add high value and work out collaborative relationships with others who have high competencies in needed areas. In some cases this involves collaboration with their students, parents, community leaders and business. In other cases, another institution (college, training organization, university) may at one moment be an educational partner; at another moment a supplier of services; and at another moment these same players could be partners in designing a new educational project or service. Collaboration is dynamic and adaptive.

Collaboration with Competing Schools in a District (the concept of strategic alliances) - the building of effective clusters - Strategic alliances began in Europe in the late 1970s and early 1980s and represented an attempt by several firms in the electronic sector to save themselves from Japanese competitors during a time when the European economies were being described as sick (suffering from "Eurosclerosis", as one writer suggested). The evolving response to this crisis was to find an efficient and effective way to collaborate with former competitors to run significant projects or create a new product without having to create a merged new company or a legal joint venture. Organizations cooperated, to a certain point, and then took the results back to their own organizations and competed. Having learned how to organize alliances with former competitors in Europe, some firms gained the confidence to explore similar alliances with the 'enemy' companies from Asia. This concept of flexible strategic alliances found its way into various sectors, and a new range of operating principles and leadership skills emerged to support such collaborative initiatives. In education, there is sometimes felt to be competition between, say Catholic and Public schools, or between public school systems and private. However, at a regional level, all are providing education that matters through people who are passionate about learning and their students. The Renaissance Leader wants to find out how collaboration with competitors could raise the performance of *all* in the region, and they will work with others to find out.

Public Good Collaboration Among Different Sectors of Society (for Profit, Non-profit, Public) - There is a need to help people see that concept of a collaborative culture is not just a nice thing to want to have, it is essential for the wellbeing of communities. It has become critical for economic success and social wellbeing. Many profit making companies are now seeing this collaboration as being essential for maintaining quality of life in their communities, which is essential for the economic well being of the company and for its ability to attract top level employees. Also, this collaboration offers employees of for-profit companies great opportunities to develop badly needed leadership skills (team building, relationship building, etc.) and offers their employees opportunity to build citizenship skills—companies can't do it easily. What could a school or school system do with volunteer labour from corporations and non profits; what projects could they lead, what teaching activities could they engage in that would make a difference to the students in a school or group of schools? How can the strengths of fundamentally different organizations be harnessed in the service of learning?

New Collaborative Roles Between Employer and Employee - The new realities of a fast changing, highly competitive global knowledge economy have put severe new pressures on the conventional long term employee/employer relationship. It is now more difficult for employers to offer secure long term employment, yet more than ever they need a commitment from employees to work as if the school was their own school – they need a sense of ownership and commitment at the level of the school as an organization. All this has led to new tensions between employers, their teachers, and other adults working in the school system and has begun to inspire the creation of quite different collaborative arrangements between them. Collaboration is no longer a 'soft', HR related idea – it's a driver for building sustained, focused performance improvement in schools. Renaissance Leaders understand this and actively model collaborative behavior. Where the leader is the representative of the employer, they act so as to build this sense of ownership and commitment.

The Six Practices of Renaissance Leaders

There are a great many factors which shape effective leadership within a school system or school as an organization, but six key characteristics stand out as necessary conditions for Renaissance Leadership. Murgatroyd and Simpson (2010)[x] studied other leadership models and reviewed a total of thirty six leadership competencies which we found dominated the extensive leadership literature. They reflected on what this meant for their view of leaders in these renaissance times and identified six practices (not traits) which reflect the observed behaviour of Renaissance Leaders. These are:

Practice personal mastery

They have high integrity and view self-awareness as a prerequisite for leadership. They work hard to develop their capacity to innovate, and to inspire others to join them in making the world a better place. They are people others want to follow, since they show by example, integrity, honesty, passion and commitment.

Apply a glocal mindset

They have a keen sense of history and seek a holistic understanding of changes taking place on a global scale. They use this global perspective as they address local challenges and seize opportunities (global and local – hence "glocal"). In education, they are aware of key developments which make a difference to the lives, performance and well-being of students and teachers and bring this awareness to their daily practice. They recognize that you cannot simply import a solution from one country and apply it to another, but they do understand that "not everything has to be invented here".

Accelerate cross-boundary learning

They constantly seek to satisfy an intense curiosity about every facet of human life, past and present, scientific and artistic, technical and social. They guide others in distilling meaning from a morass of information, and efficiently apply their learning in creative ways to
nurture innovation and drive improved performance. They don't just read and look at educational literature or attend conferences about school improvement – they try to learn about innovation, performance improvement and change from all sectors and are able to translate this work

so that it has meaning for teachers, students, parents and others.

Think back from the future

They are readily able to imagine and articulate alternate futures and work back from there – connecting with lessons from the past to better understand the present and choose among possible paths to the future they see. They are not 'locked in' to the present, but can see the future of schooling in their district clearly and steer a path working back from that future to the present. They can articulate the future as a vision for students, for learning and for the school. They can make this vision real for teachers, students and parents.

Lead systemic change

They are systems thinkers who seek out patterns, interconnections and interdependencies. They are skilled in seeking common ground and nurturing productive collaboration across diverse parts of a system – be it their own school, a school district, the education sector, a community, a network – to solve complex problems and drive large-scale change. They know how to make change happen and are used to dealing with the 'ups and downs' of the change and transformation process (see Chapter 1). They inspire followership and know how to start a movement.

Drive performance with a passion

They care that their leadership makes a substantive and sustainable difference, and are relentless in their commitment to performance. They articulate clear (and high) expectations of themselves and others, create focused strategies for innovating to achieve these ends, and are disciplined about assessing progress. They know how to use evidence to support improvement and instill in all who work with them not just a focus on outcome, but the passion and pleasure of achievement. They know how to celebrate success and build momentum based not on rhetoric but on results. They make a tangible difference.

These six characteristics are not listed in order of importance nor are they intended to be complete – it is the list that Murgatroyd and Simpson arrived at on this stage of their expedition into the process of leadership. This list can be refined, or some key characteristics can be added, but the 'feel' of this list and its focus reflects what it will take to lead in this 'in between time'.

Some have observed that the key characteristics of renaissance Leaders are deceptively simple to list but difficult to practice daily. Others have suggested that keeping the list of six characteristics close to hand helps them be better leaders daily. Our intent, in offering this thinking, is to challenge people to think about a simple question: "What kind of leadership does a perpetually innovative school - a renaissance school - need, and how can the key characteristics of these leaders best be captured?"

Necessary Conditions for Perpetual Innovation in Schools

At the heart of the thinking behind this chapter is the idea of constant change and improvement as a condition of twenty first century organizations. Communities change, organizations change, cultures develop and technology emerges. While some things remain constant, other aspects of life change all the time. The challenge is to find those points of change – those innovation opportunities – which create the chance to make significant and sustainable differences to the well-being of students, both in terms of their personal well-being and learning. The innovation process and the leadership that supports it need to focus on making mindful innovation work.

There are some necessary conditions for the school to act as a focus for innovation in the way that is outlined in this chapter. That is, a school, not a district or region or nation should be the focus for innovation. Innovation that works catches fire and is put to use at a system level only when the passion of teachers and the support of those in positional authority makes such developments possible.

There are five conditions that need to be in place at the systems level to enable effective innovation within the school. These are:

1. **Schools are recognized as the key decision centres within a district or system in which they operate.** That is, they can act quickly and effectively in support of

innovation without layers of permission or approval. In the Canadian system, for example, it is the school *not* the central office that should be enabling innovative activities. The role of the Superintendent is that of servant leader – enabling, encouraging, and easing the way. It should also be clear that "no one size fits all" – that schools have a lot of similarity between them, but it is their differences that will provide fertile ground for innovation. Unique high performing schools, not "bog standard schools" are what we should be looking for.

2. **Schools are resourced for the work they are asked to do and these resources are stable**. The cry from school systems for a basic planning period of 3-5 years of rolling, stable funding is a cry for help. Schools cannot innovate if they do not know from year to year what their resource base will be. It's inefficient and ineffective. What schools need is a degree of certainty about base funding and people resources.

3. **Investment in professional development and planning time**. Teachers, as professionals at the leading edge of learning developments, need time to plan, research and prepare. In high performing school systems this time is used for innovation, both small and large scale. Teachers cannot be expected to fully leverage new models of learning or new technology without first being able to look at and review the potential of these approaches and resources. We would not tolerate a doctor who has not spent considerable time keeping up with current

developments in medicine or who did not engage in professional development. It is no different for a professional teacher. The balance between time in class and time to prepare and innovate needs to be right.

4. **Support for risk taking**. The idea that "you can take as many risks as you like as long as they are 100% successful" is not an idea that sits well if innovation is the agenda. All innovation is a risk. Sometimes a great idea will not work. Good schools will make honest mistakes. The rule here is "we tried, we learned, we moved on and the students are fine". A former Minister of Education in Alberta once complained that there were too few failures in our system in terms of approaches to learning. He was right.

5. **Recognition**. The reward and recognition mechanisms within a school and within school districts should support an agenda for innovation and change rather than inhibit it. For example, when school performance is measured on standardized tests and nothing else and where schools can be subject to "special measures" for failing to meet some arbitrary improvement target they themselves did not set, then innovation is unlikely to occur. Innovation is a risky business and successful risk taking should be rewarded through appropriate methods of recognition and reward. Many teacher reward and recognition systems, especially in the United States, are now making innovation *less* likely to occur.

When these conditions are in place and teachers are seen as instructional leaders, supported by positional leaders acting as servant leaders, then truly remarkable things can happen.

Conclusion

This is a short summary of some more substantial aspects of thinking about innovation[xi] and schooling[xii]. The idea is simple: in order to best serve the needs of students in a fast changing community, schools need to be perpetual innovators. This sounds daunting, but is in fact a reflection of what many schools actually do and do well. What is attempted here is a summary, from a leadership perspective, of how innovative schools do this so that we can better understand what it takes to be a perpetually innovative school. After all, given the changes we will face in the coming decade[xiii], the only certainty about the future is that it will require us to be innovative.

References and Notes

[i] See Abrioux, D.A.M.X. and Ferreira, F. (Editors) (2009) *Perspectives on Distance Education: Open Schooling in the 21st Century.* Vancouver: Commonwealth of Learning.

[ii] Denning, P.J. and Dunham, B. (2010) *The Innovators Way – Essential Practices for Successful Innovation.* Cambridge, MA: MIT Press.

[iii] Murgatroyd, S. and Morgan, C. (1993) *Total Quality Management and the School*. Milton Keynes: The Open University Press.

[iv] See, for example, the OECD tracking of systematic innovation in education at http://www.oecd.org/document/1/0,3746,en_2649_35845581_38777345_1_1_1_1,00.html (Accessed 21st December 2011).

[v] Denning, P.J. and Dunham, B. (2010) *The Innovators Way – Essential Practices for Successful Innovation*. Cambridge, MA: MIT Press.

[vi] See as examples of this thinking Cunningham, W. and Gresso, D.W. (1993) *Cultural Leadership: The Culture of Excellence in Education*. Needham Heights, MA: Allyn & Bacon; Larson, R.L. (1999) Changing *Schools from the Inside Out* [Second Edition]. Lancaster, PA: Technomic Publishing Inc.

[vii] For example, see Kowalski, T.J. (2010) *The School Principal: Visionary Leadership and Competent Management*. London: Routledge; Ayers, M.B. and Sommers, W.A. (2009) *The Principal's Field Manual, The School Principal as the Organizational Leader*. Thousand Oaks, CA: Sage.

[viii] Murgatroyd, S. and Simpson, D.G. (2010) *Renaissance Leadership – Rethinking and Leading the Future*. Edmonton, AB: futureTHINK Press (available at lulu.com).

[ix] Murgatroyd, S. (2011) *Rethinking Education – Learning and the New Renaissance*. Edmonton, AB: futureTHINK Press (available at amazon.com as well as lulu.com).

[x] Murgatroyd, S. and Simpson, D.G. (2010) *Renaissance Leadership – Rethinking and Leading the Future*. New York: Lulu Press.

[xi] See Simpson, D.G. and Murgatroyd, S. (2012) *Rethinking Innovation – Driving Dramatic Improvements in Organizational Performance Through Focused Innovation*. Edmonton, AB: Future THINK Press (available at amazon.com) and also Murgatroyd, S. and Simpson, D. G. (2012) *Making Innovation Work – A Field Guide for the Practice of Focused Innovation*. Edmonton, AB: futureTHINK Press (available at amazon.com)

[xii] Murgatroyd, S. (2011) *Rethinking Education – Learning and the New Renaissance*. Edmonton, AB: future THINK Press (available at amazon.com).

[xiii] Murgatroyd, S. (2012) *Rethinking the Future – Six Patterns Shaping the New Renaissance*. Edmonton, AB: futureTHINK Press (available at amazon.com).

Appendix One

Learning our Way Forward from the Inside Out:

International Perspectives on Innovation in Education

What Makes for a Great School?

Supporting the Journey from Kindergarten to Graduation

Prepared by

Stephen Murgatroyd, J-C Couture, Chris Gonnet, Pasi Sahlberg

December 2010

Chris Gonnet Passed Away in January 2011. He is greatly missed in these dialogues and conversations.

Purpose of the Dialogue

This challenge dialogue is intended as a way of generating ideas for the Alberta–Finland partnership and the meeting of this partnership planned for March 18 and 19, 2011, in Edmonton.

It is also intended to help shape the development of both the Alberta and Finnish school systems. In Alberta, where the government has recently published *Inspiring Education, Setting the Direction* and *Inspiring Action on Education,* significant change is about to occur. Finland, as it looks to its future, also envisages changes in the school system—changes aimed at maintaining the success of Finnish schools, especially with respect to ensuring that all students have equitable access to high-quality education.

Finland and Alberta are among the leading public education jurisdictions in the world with respect to performance on certain indicators.[26] Both jurisdictions seek to continuously improve— and, if necessary, transform—their school systems so as to provide for high-quality education and skills for their citizens. What drives these decisions are the socioeconomic needs of the respective societies, a commitment to social equity and a desire to provide citizens with the knowledge and skills they require to be effective citizens in a vibrant democracy. The fundamental idea of the partnership is to find a way of learning from each other so that both jurisdictions can continue to demonstrate strong success in their respective school systems.

---

[26] These are the OECD Program of International Student Assessment (PISA) scores. See http://www4.hrsdc.gc.ca/.3ndic.1t.4r@-eng.jsp?iid=82 for more information.

The Key Challenge: What Makes for a Great School?

The underlying challenge is to identify the actions necessary to improve the effectiveness, efficiency and focus of school systems in Alberta and Finland during the next five years. That is, given that both systems have demonstrated levels of effectiveness and performance, what changes need to be made to achieve the following objectives:

- Leverage early childhood education?
- Sustain effective school performance?
- Enhance the level of student engagement and commitment to education?
- Tackle some of the issues in the education systems of Alberta and Finland that are well documented and researched?
- Provide a platform for developing an educational system that supports public education, professional teachers, mindful teaching and engaged learners?

Background

Here are some observations about Alberta and Finland that will provide some context for the discussion that follows:

1. Alberta is a predominantly public school system. While some charter and for-profit schools operate in Alberta, most K to 12 students attend a public or a publicly funded Catholic school. The government has no plans to change the balance of public, charter and private schools.

2. Finland also has a predominantly public school system. Founding a new private comprehensive school in Finland requires a political decision by the Council of State. When founded, private schools receive a State grant comparable to that given to municipal schools of the same size. However, private schools are prohibited from charging tuition fees and are obliged to admit all pupils on the same basis as the corresponding municipal school. Existing private comprehensive schools are mostly faith-based or Steiner schools.
3. Finland ranks high in the world on key Program of International Student Assessment (PISA) indicators and leads Canada in the PISA data. It is the only jurisdiction in the world to have maintained a significant lead in every administration of PISA. It is a nation committed to learning.
4. Despite its success, Alberta faces a number of challenges, among them are the following:
    a. *Alberta has a high level of drop out at the high school level.* Overall, 11.3 percent of students drop out in Alberta, which is tied with Quebec for second place behind Manitoba. In cities, the dropout rate is 9.9 percent (Alberta is third after Manitoba and Quebec), in small towns, 17 percent (first among all provinces) and in rural areas, 21.7 percent (first among all provinces).
    b. *Alberta has the lowest high-school-to-postsecondary transition rate of all provinces.* Only 48 percent of high school students go on to postsecondary education within four years of leaving high school. The national average is 62 percent.
    c. *Literacy levels among employees are problematic.* A 2006 study of the workforce (2.1 million persons) revealed that some

850,000 employees (40 percent of those employed) have a level of functional literacy below that required for the positions they occupy.

d. *Poor performance of First Nations and Métis students.* In the past three years, fewer than 15 percent of Grade 9 students in band-operated schools and fewer than 50 percent of First Nations students in other school systems met the acceptable standard in mathematics, science and social studies. So serious are these issues that the minister of education intervened in the Northland School Division in 2010 because of poor performance. Completion rates for Aboriginal students in Alberta's postsecondary system are also low: 42 percent as compared to 60 percent for the non-aboriginal students who attend colleges and universities in Alberta.

e. *Significant erosion in support to students with special needs.* In 2009, 41 percent of teachers reported that services and support for special needs students had declined in comparison to previous years.[27]

f. *Levels of student engagement in learning are low.* A study by the Metiri Group (U.S.) suggests that, on average, student engagement in their junior and senior high school work is less than 20 percent. Fifty-one percent are tactically involved, 21 percent are compliant, 5 percent are withdrawn and 3 percent are defiant. Data for Alberta from a number of masters and doctoral studies show a similar pattern.

g. *Teacher turnover remains a concern.* Average teacher turnover in Alberta is 38 percent over a four-year period.

---

[27] Source: Alberta Teachers' Association (2010) *Looking Forward—Emerging Trends and Strategic Possibilities for Enhancing Teaching and Learning in Alberta Schools, 2009–12*. Edmonton, AB, page 9.

In other words, just 62 percent of teachers remain in the classroom four years after they began. Teaching (with the exception of those who teach students with special needs) is no longer considered a "top ten" Canadian job.[28] One third of new teachers express the view that they will leave the profession within five years of starting their first teaching position.

h. *The quality of the physical infrastructure for education is declining.* Each year the government assesses the fitness of Alberta school buildings, rating them on a simple scale from "good" to "poor." Since 2005, the number in the "fair" category has increased (from 25 percent to 29 percent), while the number in the "good" category has declined (from 73 percent to 67 percent).[29]

i. *Technology adoption levels are modest.* Some 50 percent of Alberta school teachers use technology regularly and appropriately in their lessons,[30] though recent research suggests that getting past this number will require significant investments in professional development and a freeing up of curriculum demands on teachers.[31]

j. *Employers are becoming less satisfied with the outcomes of Alberta's investments in education.* In the tri-annual survey of employer satisfaction with graduates (including apprenticeship graduates) of the postsecondary system,

---

[28] See http://www.alec.co.uk/free-career-assessment/top-10-most-popular-careers.htm for details. Accessed on June 5th 2010.

[29] Source: Government of Alberta (2009) *Measuring Up—Progress Report on the Government of Alberta Business Plan.*

[30] Murgatroyd, S. and Couture, J-C (2010) *Using Technology to Support Real Learning First in Alberta Schools*. Edmonton, AB: The Alberta Teachers' Association.

[31] Metiri Group and the University of Calgary (2009) *Emerge—One to One Lap Top Learning Initiative: Year One Report*. Edmonton, AB: Government of Alberta, Ministry of Education.

satisfaction declined from 94 percent in 2005/06 to 88 percent in 2007/08.[32]
5. Finland, one of the world's leading education systems, also has a number of challenges, among them are the following:
   a. *The cost structure of the education system.* Financial constraints in post-recession Finland have affected the education system. Schools are being challenged to become more productive, in some cases by reducing their special education and counseling services or by increasing class size.
   b. *The balance of the school curriculum.* In light of the skills demanded for the Finnish economy, creativity and physical education are being downplayed.
   c. *The balance between school-based curriculum development and the role of the government in prescribing the curriculum.* There is a growing debate in Finland about where the locus of control over the curriculum should reside.
   d. *Adjusting Finland's education system to the requirements of the EU's competency-based qualifications structure, as outlined in the EU's qualifications framework.* The framework calls for more broadly based skills, especially in vocational education.
   e. *Ensuring social inclusion.* The challenge for Finland is striving to maintain not only high student performance but also an equitable education system. (Finland currently has one of the most equitable education systems in the world.)
   f. *Leveraging technology for effective instruction and increasing the use of technology for problem-solving and project-based learning.*

---

[32] Source: Government of Alberta (2009) *Measuring Up—Progress Report on the Government of Alberta Business Plan*.

g. *Rethinking the mix between vocational education and academic education.* Finland is looking to find a better balance between vocational content and academic requirements, a challenge that Alberta shares.
6. Schools in both Alberta and Finland are governed by a model that recognizes the significant role that locally elected bodies play, under the general direction of the government, in managing education. Both jurisdictions, though for different reasons, share the challenge of achieving a balance between the three domains of governance: provincial/national, school jurisdiction and the school itself.
7. Both Alberta and Finland have real concerns about resources:
   a. The costs, quality and value of teacher education and professional development.
   b. The costs, effectiveness and model for supporting students with special needs.
   c. The costs of and return on investment for educational technology.
   d. The costs and value of administrative reporting and accountability.
   e. The costs and nature of governance.
8. Alberta and Finland differ significantly in the recognition they accord to teaching as a profession:
   a. In Finland, teaching is a highly regarded profession for which there is great demand and a long-term commitment. In Alberta, teaching is increasingly regarded as a transitional profession. Many trained teachers choose either not to enter the profession or to leave after teaching for a few years.
   b. In Finland, teachers do not teach as many hours in the day as do Alberta teachers. They spend the extra time developing curriculum, planning lessons and

collaborating with other teachers on learning strategies to assist students experiencing learning challenges.
   c. In Finland, teachers have significant control over what they teach and how they teach. In Alberta, the curriculum is highly specified by the Curriculum Branch of the Government of Alberta's Ministry of Education (select teachers are highly engaged in developing curriculum at this jurisdictional level) and have some control over how they teach. In Finland, the ministry specifies a framework for curriculum, but teachers have significant opportunities to add to the "what" and "how" of their teaching.
9. Alberta intends to adopt a new *School Act* in 2011, which will initiate several reforms to education, among them are the following:
   a. The school-leaving age will increase from 16 to 17.
   b. The focus will shift from classroom-based learning for a fixed number of hours of instruction per credit to a more flexible form that will enable students to work at different paces. Not all credit will be classroom based.
   c. A broader-based model of governance will be introduced into the existing structure of school boards.
   d. Bureaucracy will be reduced.
   e. The focus will shift away from time spent in the classroom for credit to a competency-based framework linked to an understanding of 21st century skills: literacy; numeracy; critical thinking and problem solving; creativity and innovation; social responsibility and cultural, global and environmental awareness; communications; digital literacy; lifelong learning, self-direction and personal management; and collaboration and leadership.

Eight Key Challenges

1. Rethinking Governance

Both Alberta and Finland are rethinking the relationship between three levels of decision-making with respect to students and learning: (1) the role of government in framing, shaping and deciding matters of curriculum, assessment and standards; (2) the role of locally elected officials (school trustees in Alberta and municipal government in Finland) in managing resources, connecting schools to the community and ensuring that stakeholders are engaged in strategy and evaluative activities; and (3) the level of autonomy that schools are permitted in hiring teachers, shaping curriculum, assessment, evaluation and strategy. The OECD analysis strongly suggests that getting this balance right is a necessary condition for high performance outcomes.[33]

Interestingly, Finland is considering strengthening the role of the national government at the very moment when Alberta is looking at reducing the role of government and giving school boards and schools more independence.

Alberta is also looking to strengthen the involvement of the community in the governance of their schools. In other words, without changing the legal structure of its 61 school boards that have locally elected trustees, Alberta wishes to add governance models that encourage local stakeholders to become more

---

[33] See OECD PISA Study School Factors Related to Quality and Equity (2000) to at http://www.oecd.org/dataoecd/15/20/34668095.pdf accessed October 5th 2010.

engaged. These models include forming community councils for groups of schools and linking youth councils to specific schools.

Assumptions:
1. The government needs to set direction and provide sufficient guidance in terms of expectations (curriculum frameworks) and standards (suggested outcomes) without being directive to the point of de-professionalizing teachers and trying to run the schools from a bureaucratic base. Finding the balance between "framing and shaping" and "telling and directing" is difficult. Few governments think they have this right.
2. The government also has to assure the public that its investments in education are: (a) appropriate in terms of level and targeting of investment; (b) efficient and effective in how they are used; and (c) conducive to an environment in which every student has equitable access to and a chance to succeed in public education.
3. Locally elected officials are responsible for building, maintaining and supporting schools in their district that are safe, that provide appropriate education, that meet the community's expectations and that produce results demonstrating both proficient students and a high degree of equity between schools.
4. Locally elected officials are also responsible for hiring, developing and supporting teachers and other professional and semi-professional personnel who provide and support education. In Alberta, they are also responsible for determining pay and working conditions.

5. Local district leaders are responsible for encouraging and enabling innovation and supporting the development of the "system" of schools locally.
6. Parent councils and local community organizations can also provide valuable guidance to schools in terms of setting strategic priorities, focus and development.
7. Schools are responsible for providing high-quality educational opportunities and experiences that engage learners in the work of learning, require learning performance and ensure the development of social and emotional intelligence (character).
8. Schools are responsible for turning curriculum expectations into learning opportunities, evaluating student progress and assuring stakeholders that resources are being used efficiently and effectively and that the school is engaged with the community.
9. Professional teacher and administrator associations have a critical role to play in supporting the professional growth of teachers by: (a) ensuring that high-quality teachers enter the profession; (b) undertaking research; (c) providing professional development and other support; and (d) encouraging members to engage in critical self-reflection.
10. Professional associations have a key role in encouraging and enabling the development of effective schools, effective teachers and meaningful curriculum.
11. Professional associations need to represent teachers when they are challenged or threatened by political circumstance or challenged in terms of their professional integrity.

Other key stakeholders—parents, students and local businesses—also play a critical role, but are not directly involved in the balance of power and authority.

Here is what the Government of Alberta means by shared governance:

> While traditionally thought of approaches to "ownership" still apply to the system (i.e., teachers are responsible for their classroom, principals are responsible for their school, etc.), realizing a new vision for governance will mean greater commitment to cross-sectoral collaboration between education, health and social agencies as well as not-for-profit organizations. The student voice will be listened to and considered in decision making. *Approaches to governance which are more collaborative, balanced between the provincial government and local school authorities, and which reflect the unique needs of local communities, will be explored.* Building on our current model of elected school boards to strengthen the local democratic process might involve *enhanced governance at the local level through, for example, community or volunteer appointments to ensure balanced Aboriginal representation on a board responsible for a large number of Aboriginal students or which has a tuition agreement with a First Nation* (emphasis added).

2. Making Learning Meaningful: The "Personalization" of Learning

"Personalized learning," which is informing much thinking about the future of school systems, can mean a number of things:

1. *Curriculum designed uniquely for each learner*: This approach likely involves customizing learning, based on an assessment of the learner's needs, learning style and capacities. Although some special needs students may receive this form of instruction, it is unlikely to be widespread and available to all students in a public education system.
2. *A personal route through curriculum choices linked to interests, career planning and skills.* In this approach, students would choose courses that reflect their interests and personality. Finland introduced this innovation into its high schools about a decade ago.
3. *One-to-one instruction:* This approach involves ensuring that learners receive personal instruction for each subject. Such an approach is unlikely in a public education system.
4. *Online learning, anytime, anywhere*: This approach involves e-learning and is not necessarily personalized. Some school systems consider e-learning as a way of personalizing education, especially when learners can start any course at any time and take the exam or be assessed whenever they feel ready.
5. *Work-based learning credits plus credits from completed school or non-school courses equals a high school diploma or matriculation*: This approach allows high school students who have paying jobs to receive credit both for their school work and for their work-based learning. As a result, their learning is connected to their personal choices.
6. *Challenged-based learning credits:* In this approach, learners, when they feel ready, ask to be assessed and, if they succeed on the assessment, receive credit. At that point, they have learned what they need to be successful.
7. *Changing the pace of learning:* Learners are allowed to learn at their own pace and to ask for an assessment at any time.

8. *Learning linked to styles*: This approach is a form of differentiated instruction in which learning is linked to different learning styles. The same objectives are achieved through a variety of learning routes.
9. *Differential supports for learning*: Almost all "credited" learning (learning for credit) is overseen by teachers. However, there are others in the community with significant knowledge and skills (including musicians, artists, artisans, craftsmen and women, culinary artists) who could make learning possible. Why not permit them to offer instruction and allow learners to have it recognized on their profile?

To sum up, personalized learning has these characteristics:
- Students progress in programs at a pace that suits their needs and enhances their success.
- Students build on their individual strengths and achievements, pursue their passions and interests, and learn in ways that are consistent with their individual learning styles.
- Barriers to learning are reduced by allowing more flexible hours of instruction and schedules.
- Students not only have access to a greater variety of learning experiences that include and extend beyond traditional education settings but also benefit from increased community involvement in their learning.
- Multidisciplinary learning teams comprising teachers, teacher assistants, health professionals, social workers, community members and parents provide "wraparound" supports and services to optimize student success.
- Students contribute to diverse learning communities in which the social component of learning and the development and sharing of knowledge is central to their educational experience.

- Technology and community-based activities are used to enrich learning experiences and enable students to apply their learning in real-life contexts.
- There is more emphasis on assessment *for* learning (that is, an ongoing exchange between students and teachers about the progress that the student is making in achieving clearly specified outcomes).
- Students are lifelong learners who thrive in, and adapt to, a complex and rapidly changing world.

Alberta could adopt the model of the Finnish high school that is characterized by shorter courses, a high degree of student choice over when they study and with whom, and a credit-based system as opposed to grade-level learning. Finland could consider changing its vocational education schools to the more integrated approach to vocational education taken in Alberta.

Assumptions:
1. Personalized learning means giving students more options to obtaining a high school diploma or matriculation.
2. Personalized learning means more opportunities to pace when study occurs and when assessment occurs. Students can ask for an assessment when they feel ready to do so. As a result, learning is no longer linked to "time served in the classroom" but to outcomes.
3. Personalized learning requires a significant investment in counseling and guidance.
4. Learners can study courses with minimum prerequisites.
5. Learners can gain credit toward their schooling from a variety of sources: International Baccalaureate, company-based training, college or university credit and music certification programs (such as those offered by the Royal Academy of Music).

6. Learners develop a learning portfolio that can be used to gain admission to university or college.
7. Students collaborate and have a voice in how, where, when and the rate at which they learn. They are also responsible for their choices.
8. All students are empowered to participate in self-reflection and evaluation throughout their education.

3. Social Inclusion and Inclusive Education

The challenge in both Finland and Alberta is to ensure that students have equal access to, and an equal chance to succeed in, high-quality education. These two conditions are important. Having access but not the ability to succeed creates a "revolving door" for failure. The critical condition for success of an education system is that resources are applied differentially (recognizing constraints) to ensure that all students have the opportunity to achieve their potential in the public school system. Differential resource allocation would apply to Aboriginal students in Alberta, to the Sami people of northern Finland and to any students who have complex needs or learning disabilities.

Finland performs remarkably well with respect to inclusivity. The difference in outcome between schools (as measured by PISA) is less than the difference in outcome within schools. Alberta is another story: some schools perform considerably better than others in terms of outcomes. School choice is a real social issue.

Assumptions:
1. All decisions are based on the needs and interests of students.
2. Expectations are high for all students, and a number of pathways are used to ensure that they succeed. Learning is personalized.
3. Outcomes in the programs of study are the starting point for planning instruction for students. Although the process will vary depending on the individual, the outcome is what matters.
4. Programs of study are complemented with a continuum of supports and services. Classrooms, schools, school authorities and a specialist community are equipped to ensure that students have their needs met.
5. Programs of study and measures of achievement will continue to be accessible to all students.
6. School-based expertise is augmented by current research and new technologies to support teachers.
7. Teachers have resources and tools to support them in using the programs of study in more robust ways to address the diverse learning needs of all students.
8. Accessible learning resources are available so that students are provided with learning opportunities that address their interests, strengths and needs.
9. Students demonstrate their learning in multiple ways, including through refined assessment strategies that measure their progress and growth.
10. Principals lead in creating positive learning cultures in which all students and staff feel welcomed and supported.
11. Teachers are skilled in collaborating effectively with parents, principals, teacher assistants, psychologists and other specialists.

12. Parents are included as important and respected members of their child's learning team.

Alberta has a long way to go to ensure equity of access *and success* in education. Finland, which has done much to reduce inequities between schools, still has much to do to reduce differences in performance and outcome *within* schools. Social inclusion is a major objective of the education system in the United Kingdom (in the terms outlined here), but that country's progress has been problematic for a variety of reasons.

Achieving social inclusion is a challenge, especially in the area of special education. In 2010, the Government of Alberta published *Setting the Direction*, which outlines a new approach to special education, one involving a shift from a medical model in which students are categorized by the definition of their "condition" to a model that seeks to identify capabilities and possibilities. Such an approach involves the following requirements:

1. Collaboration of the deepest kind between parents and providers.
2. Customizing and personalizing curriculum and learning to take into account the potential of, and constraints faced by, the learner.
3. Using technology to render learning resources accessible.
4. Significant training and developmental support for teachers.
5. Additional capacities in classrooms to support learning and teaching, including the employment of learning coaches.

Although social inclusion is a common policy objective in developed countries, few achieve it.

4. A Relevant and Meaningful Curriculum

The Grade 7 curriculum in Alberta has more than 1,300 objectives that are to be taught in 182 days. The equivalent curriculum in Finland has less than half this number of curriculum outcomes to be taught in considerably fewer classroom hours.

A great deal of the curriculum at the high school level in Alberta is driven by the requirements of postsecondary educational institutions, especially colleges and universities. Yet less than half of the students who attend high schools in Alberta go on to attend universities or colleges, and many of those who do will not complete year one of their college or university program (the current estimate is that 15 percent drop out before the end of year one). The curriculum is being driven by needs that do not reflect the needs of the majority of those attending school or the majority of those who employ them.

In its decennial studies of skill demands, the OECD shows that the demand for skills has shifted from routine cognitive skills and technical education to an emphasis on social skills and advanced problem-solving/cognitive skills.[34]

---

[34] See OECD Skills Project reports since 1990. For example, http://www.slideshare.net/OECDPISA/oecd-skills-project-4312560.

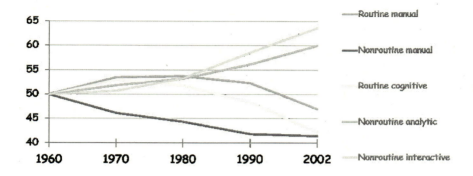

This shift in skills, coupled with the global war for talent, requires jurisdictions to rethink the focus of their curriculum and adopt a different approach to the process of learning. No one is suggesting doing away with courses such as history, social studies, sciences, math, technology and the arts. However, how these courses are experienced needs to change.

Twenty-first century skills are generally assumed to include the following abilities:
- Critical thinking and problem solving
- Creativity and innovation
- Social responsibility and cultural, global and environmental awareness
- Communication
- Digital literacy
- Lifelong learning, self-direction and personal management
- Collaboration and leadership

The curriculum base is depicted in the following chart.

Digital Age Literacy
- Basic scientific, economic and technological literacies
- Visual and information literacies
- Multicultural literacies and global awareness

Inventive Thinking
- Adaptability, managing complexity and self-direction
- Curiosity, creativity and risk taking
- Higher-order thinking and sound reasoning

Engaged, Informed and Skilled Citizens

Effective Communication
- Teaming, collaboration and interpersonal skills
- Personal, social and civic responsibility
- Interactive communication

High Productivity
- Prioritizing, planning and managing for results
- Effective use of real world tools
- Ability to produce relevant, high-quality products
- Ability to innovate through continuous improvement

Yet these so-called 21st century skills need to link to more traditional high school subject matter such as history, mathematics, physics, chemistry, biology and social studies. The knowledge underlying 21st century skills may not differ significantly from that involved in 20th century skills, but the pedagogy involved in imparting this knowledge and understanding may be very different. The emphasis on collaborative team-based work, civic responsibility and global activity all suggest a renewed pedagogy.

Assumptions:
1. At the heart of 21st century skills is the ambition that all students will achieve digital and mathematical literacy as well as Level 3 literacy in the international standard of literacy for the knowledge economy.[35]
2. There are several routes to ensuring that students leave school with the required skills. There is no "silver bullet" or "right way." Many of these skills can be obtained by studying such courses as science, history, language arts and social studies. In acquiring skills for the 21st century, students need access to different ways of knowing and a foundation in a core curriculum.
3. The process of learning is as important as the content of learning. Mindful teaching should be the support for effective learning.
4. Different students need to experience different kinds of teaching. Visual learners differ from linear learners who differ from exploratory learners, and so on. Differentiated

---

[35] **Adult literacy levels:**
Level 5: Very strong skills—able to find information in dense text and make high-level inferences or use specialized background information.
Level 4: Strong skills—able to integrate and synthesize information from complex or lengthy passages.
Level 3: Adequate skills for coping in a complex advanced society. Equivalent to the skill level required for high school completion and college entry.
Level 2: Weak skills—can deal with simple clearly laid out material. May be able to cope with everyday demands but will have difficulty with new situations.
Level 1: Very poor skills—may not be able to determine the correct dosage from the label on a medicine bottle.

instruction is not an optional but an essential feature of a 21st century classroom.
5. Curriculum is the product of a central framework (determined by the government) and a local interpretation of that framework (determined by professional teachers).
6. Skills for the 21st century have a lot in common with 20th century skills.[36] The focus is on developing capable citizens who have a passion for learning and have skills relevant to their ambitions and intent.

5. Appropriate Technology for Learning

Technology can be a significant tool for accelerating and supporting learning, provided that the tool is seen as just that: a support, a resource and an opportunity, not a substitute for relationship-driven learning.

Finland has undertaken several studies on how technology can be leveraged to advance the learning agenda of the nation.[37] The goal of the *ICTs at School's Everyday Life* project (supported by the Ministry of Transport and Communications, the Ministry of Education and the Finnish National Board of Education in cooperation with industry and commerce) is not only to inform schools and educational administration about the latest developments in ICT but also to develop multiple ways of

---

[36] See http://www.youtube.com/watch?v=8_ehGLqzBVM.

[37] See a summary of developments in *OECD Study on Digital Learning Resources As Systematic Innovation—Country Case Study Report on Finland*, available at http://www.oecd.org/dataoecd/47/1/42159200.pdf. Accessed on October 3, 2010.

applying ICT to education. More specifically, the project aims to improve understanding and practice in the following areas:
- ICT tools, infrastructure and usability
- Learning environments and pedagogical models (for example, using social media and mobile learning as part of the school's everyday life)
- Creating content and learning materials
- Developing school communities and supporting professional development and collaboration
- Developing public–private partnership models

The results are expected in 2011. Work is underway in 12 Finnish schools, and 20 schools are involved in the research consortium.

The Government of Alberta has spent close to $2 billion on educational technology for schools since 1998. This money has been spent on hardware, software and professional development. Although the use of technology continues to grow, its application has presented a number of challenges that Murgatroyd and Couture (2010) explored in a paper entitled <u>Using Technology to Support Real Learning First in Alberta Schools.</u>[38] Based on a critique of technology adoption and implementation, Murgatroyd and Couture suggest that Alberta needs to do the following:

1. Create a learning consortium to review leading practices and test new practices with respect to renewing and transforming the curriculum.

---

[38] Available at http://www.teachers.ab.ca/SiteCollectionDocuments/ATA/Publications/Research-Updates/PD-86-17%20Using%20Technology%20to%20Support%20RLF%20in%20Alberta%20Schools.pdf. Accessed October 6, 2010.

2. Establish a new targeted fund (comparable to AISI but with more focus on local decision making) to help transform 10 schools, in partnership with their respective communities, into major centres of professional development, research and innovation.
3. In consultation with the education partners, establish priorities with respect to future government investments in digital technology.
4. Redesign, in consultation with the faculties of education, the Association and other education partners, Alberta's current programs of study.
5. Work with the education partners to enhance teachers' leadership skills.
6. Ensure that every community in Alberta has broadband access, whether wired or wireless, to the Internet.
7. In collaboration with jurisdictions, universities, colleges and the Association, fund field research to determine the kinds of technologies that optimize student learning.

Many claims are made for technology, and many vendors are competing for what they see as lucrative markets. More significantly, students see certain technologies (searching, texting, tweeting, social media and music) as utility services, not as optional services. They are increasingly disappointed by the general failure to integrate technology into the learning process.

Assumptions:
1. Technology is not a substitute for learning based on student–teacher interactions.

2. Technology can be a source for knowledge and information, provided that learners have developed the skills of discrimination and critical thinking. Not all information available online is reliable or complete.
3. Digital devices—especially mobile devices such as the iPad and Smartphones—can be powerful tools for accessing knowledge. Social networking tools can be used to facilitate project-based learning and learning situations that require the co-creation of knowledge.
4. The digital media is rapidly replacing textbooks. Many of these services permit registered teachers to add local content, an arrangement that allows school systems to improve the access that students have to high quality and affordable learning resources.
5. E-learning (online learning) is a proven method of offering high-quality instruction. Many students, especially high school students, find this form of learning as good as (and, in some cases and for some students, better than) classroom instruction, especially in subjects in which they have a high degree of commitment and interest. The evidence is clear that there is no significant difference between learning outcomes from e-learning as opposed to classroom learning.
6. For technology to be used effectively as part of the process of learning, teachers need support and professional development. Reading the manual is not enough.
7. Learning in the 21st century without using technology is not something most students can imagine or will find acceptable.

8. Technology changes quickly, and schools need to be able to respond flexibly to opportunities as they occur.
9. To adopt technology successfully, school systems must share effective practices.
10. Giving technology to schools because the government thinks ``it will be good for them`` is a great way to satisfy the needs of vendors but is unlikely to improve learning outcomes or enhance levels of student engagement.
11. Determining whether technology has been successfully adapted involves measuring: (a) levels of utilization; (b) increases in student engagement; and (c) improvements in learning outcomes. All three conditions need to be considered in assessing the efficacy of technology.
12. The digital divide is real. Some students do not have access to broadband services, and many cannot afford the latest technology. If equity is a driving principle, the digital divide must be addressed.

6. Moving from Accountability to Assurance

In an effort to hold schools accountable for performance, governments in a number of OECD countries adopted an approach that tested students at key stages of their schooling. In Alberta, this approach has resulted in standardized testing for all students in Grades 3, 6 and 9 as well as for all students completing their high school diploma. Finland has no similar testing regime during the normal period of schooling. Instead, students' progress is measured by accumulating credits.

However, Finland does have matriculation examinations that provide a bridge between the school and postsecondary education.[39] Here's how the National Board of Education of Finland describes the matriculation examinations:

> The examination consists of at least four tests; one of them, the test in the candidate's mother tongue, is compulsory for all candidates. The candidate then chooses three other compulsory tests from among the following four tests: the test in the second national language, a foreign language test, the mathematics test, and one test in the general studies battery of tests (sciences and humanities). The candidate may include, in addition, as part of his or her examination, one or more optional tests. There is a separate assessment system for the matriculation examination. The tests are initially checked and assessed by each upper secondary school's teacher of the subject in question and finally by the Finnish Matriculation Examination Board.

Students often take additional time after completing their high school course requirements to prepare for matriculation. This matriculation process is seen as essential for the selection system for postsecondary places. There is strong competition, for example, for teacher education places, and the examination helps identify the most able students. The purpose of the examination, however, is not to assess the performance of the school system

---

[39] Universities in Finland accept applicants who have graduated from high school or upper secondary school with an IB (International Baccalaureate), EB (European Baccalaureate) or Reifeprüfung diploma (in any country offering these type of qualifications) or with a Finnish Upper Secondary School Diploma in English.

(accountability). Accountability is monitored by special studies and occasional sample-based studies of particular issues.

Finland does, however, take one external assessment very seriously—the Program of International Student Assessment (PISA), which assesses the performance of Finland's system against those of others in the OECD. Each time the assessment is undertaken (every three years), Finland appears "best in class" amongst all OECD countries. Although Alberta also ranks very high, it has adopted a completely different accountability framework than its Finnish counterpart.

More recently, a number of jurisdictions that used to use standardized testing to measure system accountability have moved away from that approach and have adopted an assurance model.

Assumptions:
1. Not all schools have the same history, resources, catchment, intake quality, levels of teacher experience and access to technology. Each school has unique characteristics.
2. Assessing students as if they were equal because they are the same age neglects the significant differences between students of the same age that result from such factors as birth order and month of birth, intelligence and ability, parental support for learning and the availability of social supports. In short, not all 11-year-olds are equal at the point of testing.
3. To be held accountable for its use of public resources and its work, a school needs to own its work: its strategic intent and purpose, its methods of teaching and its process for evaluating and supporting students.
4. Schools want to be accountable for their work and the performance of their students.
5. Schools can use sampling, teacher evaluation (if teachers are trained and supported to perform evaluations) and other measures (peer evaluation, parent evaluation, self-tests) to assess performance and progress.
6. Rather than having their performance based on a single set of measures (such as provincial achievement tests or matriculation scores), schools should develop a plan that spells out performance objectives and then report on the progress made in achieving those objectives.
7. The primary level of accountability in the school system rests with professional teachers undertaking professional student assessments.

8. School boards hold schools accountable for living up to their commitments and assurances.
9. When a school is clearly unable to meet its own commitments and intent, the school board needs to support the school in planning changes.

7. Instructional Leadership

A school is more than a place where teachers meet students and teach. It is an organization that has rules, culture, focus and a variety of other unique features. No two schools are the same, despite having similar resources and similar strategic intentions. Indeed, one of the fascinating aspects of education is how different one school can be from another.

Studies of school effectiveness conducted by David Reynolds, Sir Michael Rutter and other researchers in the early 1980s to the mid-1990s demonstrated that schools as organizations can affect student performance. Their findings appear in such books as *15,000 Hours — Secondary Schools and Their Effects on Children* (Rutter et al, 1982[40]) and *The Comprehensive Experiment* (Reynolds, Sullivan and Murgatroyd, 1987[41]). According to these authors, the key variables affecting student performance are: (1) the culture and history of the school; and (2) the style of instructional leadership exercised by the principal or head teacher. The authors concluded that these two variables accounted for between 8 and 10 percent of the difference between high- and

---

[40] Harvard University Press.
[41] Taylor & Francis.

low-performing schools. Principals and school leaders can make a big difference in the school by doing the following:
1. Shaping the experience of schooling for a generation or more of students.
2. Shaping the experience of new teachers as they begin their teaching careers.
3. Shaping the experience of teachers at each stage of their professional development.
4. Being an inspiration through their leadership and personality.
5. Enabling innovation.
6. Being efficient and effective problem solvers.
7. Shielding teachers from bureaucracy.
8. Being the voice of the school in the community.
9. Championing the school at each opportunity.
10. Making a difference to each student through their interactions with them.

The quality of instructional leadership varies both by school and by the amount of experience that the leader has. Not all principals or head teachers are "great," but a great many are. They can make a real difference in how teachers, students and others perceive the school.

Assumptions:
1. The culture of a school—its focus, the alignment of teachers and adults in the school to this focus, its processes and procedures, and the way it communicates—significantly affect learning outcomes.
2. Instructional leadership—developing excellence among teachers within the school through careful selection, support and investment in their development—is a critical component in making a good school.
3. Instructional leadership requires principals (head teachers) to focus on teaching and learning rather than on administration only. Principals need to observe teaching, give feedback and systematically develop best practices.
4. Instructional leadership is tough to do. School leaders face many competing demands on their time. However, focusing relentlessly on teaching and learning rather than on administration will almost certainly produce more gains in student performance.
5. Instructional leaders themselves require development and support. Some jurisdictions require teachers to be qualified for the work of school leadership.

8. Mindful Teaching

The key to a great high school is the quality of the teaching. Good teachers make a great deal of difference by engaging students and ennobling learning as a process. In their book *The Mindful Teacher*,[42] Elizabeth MacDonald and Dennis Shirley speak eloquently of the profound influence that teachers can have. They describe seven synergies or practices that characterize mindful teachers:

1. *Open Mindedness*: Mindful teachers engage with their students, parents and the community, find out what their students are interested in and attempt to connect the minds of their students to ideas and learning resources.
2. *Loving and Caring*: Mindful teachers genuinely care about and express appropriate affection for their students.
3. *Professional Expertise*: Mindful teachers demonstrate daily, through their knowledge and processes, their expertise as teachers, coaches, mentors and guides.
4. *Authentic Alignment*: Mindful teachers are genuinely engaged and aligned with the work of the school and express this engagement in their work with students.
5. *Integrative and Harmonizing*: Mindful teachers enable students and others to make connections, see patterns and understand the connectedness of the curriculum.
6. *Collective Responsibility*: Rather than relying on testing, mindful teachers understand that they are responsible for evaluating and enabling learning and understanding where a

---

[42] 2009, Teachers College Press.

learner is at in his or her journey toward mastering a specific subject. Although one teacher may have a piece of this puzzle, all who teach a student should work together in assessing the student and determining the next steps to take in supporting the student; Good teachers not only understand the importance of collective responsibility but act accordingly.

7. *Stopping*: Mindful teachers stop and critically reflect on their work. They also take time to care for themselves not just occasionally but daily. In other words, they attempt to achieve their own "inner balance" so that they can better support their students.

Since this book was published in 2009, many teachers have reported that, of the seven synergies, the most difficult to achieve consistently is "stopping" and finding a balance for themselves.

Assumptions:

1. The quality of teaching and student performance is strongly linked.
2. Good teaching is a function of training, professional development and day-to-day collective support and instructional leadership in a school.
3. Contrary to the popular belief that a teacher is "king or queen" in the classroom, mindful teachers are most effective when they function as part of a team working to ensure that students in their school are engaged in meaningful learning.
4. Schools that cultivate good teachers are more likely to retain those teachers than schools that don't focus on the quality of teaching.

5. Good teachers create as well as deliver. They use their own knowledge, resources and networks to create meaningful learning experiences for students, and they link these experiences to the "required" curriculum.
6. Good teachers need time to "stop" and find their own balance.

References and Notes

[i] See Abrioux, D.A.M.X. and Ferreira, F. (Editors) (2009) *Perspectives on Distance Education: Open Schooling in the 21st Century.* Vancouver: Commonwealth of Learning.

[ii] Denning, P.J. and Dunham, B. (2010) *The Innovators Way – Essential Practices for Successful Innovation.* Cambridge, MA: MIT Press.

[iii] Murgatroyd, S. and Morgan, C. (1993) *Total Quality Management and the School.* Milton Keynes: The Open University Press.

[iv] See, for example, the OECD tracking of systematic innovation in education at http://www.oecd.org/document/1/0,3746,en_2649_35845581_38777345_1_1_1_1,00.html (Accessed 21st December 2011).

[v] Denning, P.J. and Dunham, B. (2010) *The Innovators Way – Essential Practices for Successful Innovation.* Cambridge, MA: MIT Press.

[vi] See as examples of this thinking Cunningham, W. and Gresso, D.W. (1993) *Cultural Leadership: The Culture of Excellence in Education*. Needham Heights, MA: Allyn & Bacon; Larson, R.L. (1999) Changing *Schools from the Inside Out* [Second Edition]. Lancaster, PA: Technomic Publishing Inc.

[vii] For example, see Kowalski, T.J. (2010) *The School Principal: Visionary Leadership and Competent Management*. London: Routledge; Ayers, M.B. and Sommers, W.A. (2009) *The Principal's Field Manual, The School Principal as the Organizational Leader*. Thousand Oaks, CA: Sage.

[viii] Murgatroyd, S. and Simpson, D.G. (2010) *Renaissance Leadership – Rethinking and Leading the Future*. Edmonton, AB: future**THINK** Press (available at lulu.com).

[ix] Murgatroyd, S. (2011) *Rethinking Education – Learning and the New Renaissance*. Edmonton, AB: future**THINK** Press (available at amazon.com as well as lulu.com).

[x] Murgatroyd, S. and Simpson, D.G. (2010) *Renaissance Leadership – Rethinking and Leading the Future*. New York: Lulu Press.

[xi] See Simpson, D.G. and Murgatroyd, S. (2012) *Rethinking Innovation – Driving Dramatic Improvements in Organizational Performance Through Focused Innovation*. Edmonton, AB: future**THINK** Press (available at amazon.com) and also Murgatroyd, S. and Simpson, D. G. (2012) *Making Innovation Work – A Field Guide for the Practice of Focused Innovation*. Edmonton, AB: future**THINK** Press (available at amazon.com)

[xii] Murgatroyd, S. (2011) *Rethinking Education – Learning and the New Renaissance*. Edmonton, AB: future**THINK** Press (available at amazon.com).

[xiii] Murgatroyd, S. (2012) *Rethinking the Future – Six Patterns Shaping the New Renaissance*. Edmonton, AB: future**THINK** Press (available at amazon.com).